ABSINTHE

WORLD LITERATURE IN TRANSLATION

ORPHANED OF LIGHT
Translating Arab and Arabophone Migration

Edited by Graham Liddell

I0672759

ABSINTHE: World Literature in Translation is published by the
Department of Comparative Literature at the University of Michigan.

ABSINTHE: World Literature in Translation receives the generous support
of the following schools, offices, and programs at the University of Michigan:
Rackham Graduate School, Office of the Vice Provost for Global and Engaged
Education, International Institute, and the College of Literature, Science, and
the Arts.

Typesetting and Design
William Kalvin, Delmas Typesetting. Ann Arbor, Michigan delmastype.com

ISBN: 978-1-60785-820-1
ISSN: 1543-8449

https://journals.publishing.umich.edu/absinthe/
Follow us on Twitter: @AbsintheJournal

ABSINTHE 28

Editor's Acknowledgments

I send my sincere thanks to the University of Michigan's Department of Comparative Literature, which has been *Absinthe*'s home for the last eight years and whose faculty give generously of their time to provide mentorship to the graduate students who work on the journal. I am also very grateful to the Department of Middle East Studies for its financial contribution toward the production of this issue.

I am indebted to *Absinthe*'s wonderful team of managing editors, whose careful copyediting and behind-the-scenes planning helped make this issue possible. To Sara Abou Rashed: thank you for the time and effort you put into copyediting the issue's Arabic script and ensuring the accuracy of its translations. I also thank Julia Schwartz for her helpful comments on a draft of the introduction.

To David Álvarez, Khaled Mattawa, Dunya Mikhail, and Anton Shammas: thank you for recommending possible works to translate for this issue and for helping me get in contact with their authors.

On a personal note, I send my renewed appreciation to three friends who have been of regular assistance to me each time I've undertaken an Arabic-to-English translation project: Ali Harb, Aysam Iyrot, and Ammar Owaineh.

To Yopie Prins: thank you so much for encouraging me in my various translation-related pursuits throughout my time as a graduate student at Michigan. This issue of *Absinthe* would not have materialized without you.

And finally, *shukran jazeelan* to the translators and authors who contributed their work to *Absinthe* 28. Engaging with your words has made my job as an editor a true joy.

Graham Liddell

Introduction

In 2022, the world reached a dire milestone: according to the UN Refugee Agency (UNHCR), the number of displaced people around the world surpassed 100 million. To put this figure in perspective, one in every 78 people on earth has been forced to leave home on account of war, human rights abuses, food insecurity, and climate-related disasters.[1]

Scholars have pointed out that in this age of unprecedented forced displacement, asylum seeking, and unauthorized migration, it is crucial to listen to migrants and refugees and not just to commentators whose own domiciles and livelihoods are fixed and secure.[2] This push to listen is especially crucial given that the voices of those who have firsthand experience of displacement tend to be conspicuously absent from both media reports and policy debates on the subject of migration. In fact, even in their own asylum interviews, applicants for refugee status are rarely able to speak freely given the strict criteria for being granted asylum in host countries around the world.

Orphaned of Light: Translating Arab and Arabophone Migra-

---

[1] "More Than 100 Million."
[2] See, e.g., McKenzie and Triulzi, "Listening to Migrants' Narratives"; Andrews, Introduction; and Squire et al., Introduction.

tion takes a literary approach to the endeavor of listening to migrant voices. *Absinthe 28* features translations of contemporary Arabic literature—most originally published in the 21st century—on experiences of migration, broadly defined. In these works, "migration" includes but is not limited to forced displacement. It takes numerous forms and is considered from a variety of perspectives: diasporic life, undocumented labor, refugeehood, human trafficking, internal displacement, exile. The works' authors are individuals whose personal experiences of, or up-close encounters with, migration inform their writing on the subject.

Translating Migrant Voices

The call to "listen to migrant voices" should be more than a vague platitude recited in the name of inclusivity. One specific reason to emphasize the importance of detailed firsthand accounts of unauthorized migration is that in many host countries, the field of mainstream discourse about refugees and migrants is limited by "hostility themes" in which oversimplified narratives in opposition to and in defense of migrants are constantly battling each other.[3] Those on the political right tend to paint migrants as dangerous or at least burdensome, whereas liberals tend to emphasize migrants' victimhood and lack of alternatives. In this fraught discursive landscape, the fact that migrants must at times take forceful or artful action in the face of violently exclusionary border regimes becomes an opportunity for migration antagonists to demonize the newcomers. Meanwhile, many refugee advocates ignore these complex forms of migrant agency, which disrupt the simple, touching arc of tragedy and philanthropy.

Not only do asylum seekers have to contend with these diametrically opposed and flattening narratives when telling their stories to audiences in their host countries, but they also internalize some of them. With this in mind, we can understand how literature in Arabic (and other languages) on the subject of migration can serve the purpose of sorting through conflicting feelings about it, away from

---

[3] Leudar et al., "Hostility Themes."

the Western media spotlight. On the page, migrant authors can treat such thorny issues as smuggling and human trafficking, the common tactic of stretching the truth during asylum interviews, the ills of international aid, and religious fundamentalism without much fear of playing into the hands of a host country's nationalist ideologues. And the domestic popularity of Arabic literature on unauthorized migration demonstrates that the phenomenon might well be as much an object of curiosity and debate in "sending" countries as it is in "countries of reception."

Translators face a difficult question, then: If one of the purposes of Arabic migration literature is to provide a secluded venue in which to air raw emotions and express views on controversial subjects, what are the ethics of translating this literature into English? Is it possible that such translations could do more harm than good?

Khaled Mattawa, one of *Absinthe 28*'s translators, addressed a similar concern at a symposium I co-organized with him in the fall of 2021 at the University of Michigan called "Translation and the Making of Arab American Community." The interplay between Arabic and English, he said, has been "a part of mediating the Arab American experience for a long time." In the city of Dearborn, Michigan, which boasts the largest concentration of Arabs in the United States, Arab residents from various national, religious, generational, and linguistic backgrounds must "translate" their experiences not just for non-Arabs, but for *one another*—including some members of younger generations who have limited proficiency in the language. Therefore, in visiting a community like Dearborn, one enters "not a melting pot necessarily, but a market of exchanged, evolving ideas that are working toward a medium." Still, Mattawa added, there remains a palpable ambivalence over publicizing this multilingual dialogue:

> The specter that haunts this utopic state of existence where Arabic and English are kind of flourishing is the surveillance and security that is eavesdropping on these conversations. So while we come to this conversation with a lot of excitement and with a lot to learn from each other, we will not neglect the fact that we are being overheard all the time, even here.[4]

_____

[4] To watch a video recording of Mattawa's speech and the rest of the event's proceed-

It is true: government surveillance has been an unsettling, panoptic reality for Arab Americans, particularly in the years following the 9/11 attacks.[5] And in the case of unauthorized migration to Europe, long before migrants physically enter the EU, the European Border Surveillance System (Eurosur) tracks them with imaging and sensing technologies using satellites and reconnaissance aircraft.[6] Both Eurosur and the European Border and Coast Guard Agency (Frontex) sanitize their image by operating with both a policing and a humanitarian mission—keeping migrants out, yes, but also saving their lives by facilitating and conducting rescue operations and targeting violent smuggler gangs.[7] This humanitarian element might be intended to keep at bay accusations that these entities actually *bring about* migrant deaths, but scholars have nonetheless shown that by forcing unauthorized migration further underground, governments make it even more dangerous, compelling migrants to undertake darker, stormier, more remote—and thus deadlier—crossings.[8]

In light of this systematic surveillance, legitimate misgivings may arise for migrants about being translated. With this critique in mind, why take on this project of translating a collection of contemporary Arabic literary works about migration and refugeehood? A couple of factors may begin to allay concerns. First, we have, of course, received permission to translate and publish these works, and many of the authors we contacted expressed excitement for their writing to be made available to a broader, Anglophone readership. Second, there is an argument to be made that although the Arabic language can make possible the kind of non-polarized discourse that digs deep into the uncomfortable nuances of migration and migrant subjectivity, this does not mean that this discourse automatically transforms *back* into a polarized one when an Arabic work is translated into English. On the contrary, translation can create much needed open-

---

ings, visit https://sites.lsa.umich.edu/translatemidwest/2021/11/12/november-12-2021-symposium-on-translation-and-the-making-of-arab-american-community/.

[5] See, e.g., Khan and Ramachandran, "Post-9/11 Surveillance"; and Scahill and Devereaux, "Watch Commander."

[6] See Ajana, "Digital Biopolitics."

[7] Andersson, *Illegality, Inc.*, 72–73.

[8] See, e.g., De León, *Land of Open Graves*; and Albahari, *Crimes of Peace*.

ings for dialogue in otherwise deadlocked debates by introducing new, unexpected details and immersive reading experiences. But—and I stress this point—these justifications do not magically resolve the tension between the sunny view of Arabic-to-English translation as a force for greater mutual understanding, on the one hand, and the darker, more critical view of it as a kind of unwelcome surveillance, on the other.

"Orphaned of Light"

Absinthe 28's title gestures toward some of the complexity I have laid out above. "Orphaned of light" is a phrase borrowed from one of this issue's selections, a poem written by Dearborn-based writer Gulala Nouri and translated by Ali Harb. But the motif of light and darkness, often infused with a deep sense of loss, runs throughout several of the pieces featured here. In many cases, the motif takes the form of a character being deprived of—and craving—actual or metaphorical light but nonetheless taking advantage of darkness. Refugees flee dark circumstances and seek brighter futures abroad, but given the illegalized nature of their journeys across borders, most of them must make their way under the cover of darkness.

For some, even after arriving in Europe, their futures are still "bereft of light," as Rachid Niny writes in *Journal of a Clandestine Migrant*, a selection of which is translated by Angela Haddad for this issue. But the fact that Niny does not possess the proper documentation to reside legally in Spain *requires* him to operate "undercover," which, as Haddad points out, is another possible translation for the adjective in the book's title. Elsewhere, the dynamics of light and darkness are more literal. In Nisma Alaklouk's "Her, Him, and Gaza," translated by Julia Schwartz, Gaza is described as often wearing a "dark outfit—sometimes as funeral garb for the multitude of martyrs, sometimes because there wasn't enough diesel to fuel the manual electricity generator." Still, for Alaklouk's narrator, the joys of light cannot be fully appreciated in her new home in Belgium. The New Year's fireworks remind her too much of the sound of bombs falling, which she heard on a regular basis in Gaza.

The aforementioned poem by Nouri, "No Flowers on My Doorstep," contains a similar emotional contradiction. The speaker repeats the sentence "Flowers are not for me" and describes the neighborhood women who *do* keep flowers on their doorsteps as only caring about appearances while remaining ignorant of life's darker realities. And yet the speaker admits that she used to keep flowers herself but was "bereaved" of them. They were "plucked" from her and given as gifts to soldiers going off to war or laid in the caskets of those who died in battle. In those caskets, "my flowers are orphaned of light / and I am orphaned here in this house on the intersection." The refrain "flowers are not for me" thus reveals itself to be not a statement of personal taste, but rather a lament. As in the examples above, the poet's relationship with light (a condition for flowers to grow) is an ambivalent one, which connects with migrants' ambivalence about being translated. The play of light and darkness suggests a desire to be seen and to express oneself, on the one hand, and a need for privacy and even secrecy, on the other.

Side-by-Side Translation

We have attempted to further reflect this theme of revealing and concealing by presenting this issue's poetry in a side-by-side Arabic-English format. The presence of the Arabic text serves as a reminder that a translation, especially of a poem, is not a "faithful copy" of an "original," but another entry point into an expanded literary work. For Iraqi poet Dunya Mikhail, who spoke at the Arab American translation symposium, translation is not a transfer of an original poem to a new language but rather a second writing of the poem. Her bilingual poetry reading at the event was an exemplar of the way that translation can provide a multidimensional experience of a work of art that would not otherwise be possible. For Palestinian American writer Sara Abou Rashed, who translated her own poetry for this issue of *Absinthe*, the bilingual format brings out overtones of "past lives"—hers in Damascus, her grandparents' in Haifa—that she perceives amid her current experiences in the United States. She writes,

"I cannot imagine what it feels like to know only one [language], to express my thoughts in only one register, octave, rhythm, alphabet. Perhaps we—multilinguals—come to cultivate consciousnesses greater than the singularity of each of our languages."

The side-by-side format also allows us to publish works by two poets who originally wrote their poems in English. The inclusion of Arabic renderings of these English-language poems points to the fact that translation of migration literature need not—and should not—be an extractive practice by which English literature is enriched. Instead, translation must be understood as multidirectional and multifunctional. While Abou Rashed's translation of her own work into her mother tongue works primarily as a means of authentic self-expression, Mootacem Mhiri's English-to-Arabic translation of scholar and activist Becky Thompson's work accomplishes something quite different. Thompson's poetry bears witness to the experiences of refugees she met while volunteering in Greece, and Mhiri's translation makes that poetry more accessible to many of those about whom she writes.

Why Arabic?

Little of the above discussion on migrant voices, border regimes, the imagery of light and darkness, and the migrant subject's selective tendency toward revealing and concealing is specific to Arabic-speaking refugees. So why limit this issue of *Absinthe* to translations from (or to) a single language? Though Arabic may be the most widely spoken language among the world's refugees today, Arabic-speaking migrants share routes, smugglers, and refugee camps with speakers of numerous other languages: Farsi/Dari, Pashto, French, Kurmanji and Sorani (along with other dialects of Kurdish), Urdu, and many more. Why not include work translated from some of these languages as well?

One reason is simply the reality of limitations on time, resources, and foreign language skills. A more satisfying answer, however, relates to the Arab communities of Dearborn, where the University of Michigan has a campus and whose diverse stories of migration (along with those of Dearborn Heights, Hamtramck, and other cities) enrich the unique cultural character of Metro Detroit. Indeed, Arabic is the third most widely spoken language in the state of Michigan. This August, in a move that language access advocates had long been fighting for, Dearborn held its first elections for which Arabic-language ballots were provided. Though *Absinthe* has featured individual translations from Arabic in the past, this is the first issue devoted entirely to Arabic literature. For a translation journal that was founded in Detroit and was adopted by the University of Michigan, the publication of such an issue seems highly fitting, if not overdue.

A final reason to feature exclusively Arabic works in an issue on migration and displacement is the fact that since the Nakba of 1948, the Palestinian refugee has been a central figure in Arabic literature. In Arabic, the word *lāji'* (refugee) immediately conjures up thoughts and images of Palestine and its people. The works of refugee writer Ghassan Kanafani are peerless in their depiction of the plight of displaced Palestinians. In the final scene of his novel *Men in the Sun*, three refugees suffocate in the back of a lorry during a botched clandestine border-crossing attempt. This scene remains unrelentingly poignant as media reports of similar calamities appear on a painfully regular basis today. We open this issue of *Absinthe* with a lesser-known short story of Kanafani's, "The Stolen Shirt," translated by Michael Fares. Its depiction of life in a Palestinian refugee camp in the 1950s sets the stage for the more contemporary works that are featured in this issue. The story serves as a chilling reminder of the decades-long genealogy of Arab refugeehood that has continued with renewed vigor in the 21st century.

Works Cited

Ajana, Btihaj. "Digital Biopolitics, Humanitarianism and the Datafication of Refugees." In *Refugee Imaginaries*, edited by Emma Cox, Sam Durrant, David Farrier, Lyndsey Stonebridge, and Agnes Woolley, 463–479. Edinburgh: Edinburgh University Press, 2020.
Albahari, Maurizio. *Crimes of Peace: Mediterranean Migrations at the*

World's Deadliest Border. Philadelphia: University of Pennsylvania Press, 2015.

Andersson, Ruben. *Illegality, Inc.: Clandestine Migration and the Business of Bordering Europe*. Oakland: University of California Press, 2014.

Andrews, Abigail Leslie. Introduction to *Undocumented Politics: Place, Gender, and the Pathways of Mexican Migrants*, 1–27. Oakland: University of California Press, 2018.

De León, Jason. *The Land of Open Graves: Living and Dying on the Migrant Trail*. Oakland: University of California Press, 2015.

Kanafani, Ghassan. *Rijāl fi-sh-Shams* [Men in the sun]. Limassol: 2013 [1963].

Khan, Saher, and Vignesh Ramachandran. "Post-9/11 Surveillance Has Left a Generation of Muslim Americans in a Shadow of Distrust and Fear." *PBS NewsHour*, PBS, September 16, 2021. https://www.pbs.org/newshour/nation/post-9-11-surveillance-has-left-a-generation-of-muslim-americans-in-a-shadow-of-distrust-and-fear.

Leudar, Ivan, Jacqueline Hayes, Jiří Nekvapil, and Johanna T. Baker. 2008. "Hostility Themes in Media, Community and Refugee Narratives." *Discourse and Society* 19 (2): 187-221.

McKenzie, Robert Lawrence, and Alessandro Triulzi. "Listening to Migrants' Narratives: An Introduction." In *Long Journeys: African Migrants on the Road*, edited by Alessandro Triulzi and Robert McKenzie, 1–7. Leiden: Brill, 2013.

"More Than 100 Million Now Forcibly Displaced: UNHCR Report." *UN News*, June 16, 2022. https://news.un.org/en/story/2022/06/1120542.

Scahill, Jeremy, and Ryan Devereaux. "Watch Commander: Barack Obama's Secret Terrorist-Tracking System, by the Numbers." *The Intercept*, August 5, 2014. https://theintercept.com/2014/08/05/watch-commander/.

Squire, Vicki, Nina Perkowski, Dallal Stevens, and Nick Vaughan-Williams. Introduction to *Reclaiming Migration: Voices from Europe's 'Migrant Crisis,'* 1–19. Manchester: Manchester University Press, 2021.

Ghassan Kanafani

The Stolen Shirt

Translated by Michael Fares

Translator's Reflection

What follows is a translation of a short story written by Ghassan Kanafani in 1958, titled "The Stolen Shirt." Although among his relatively lesser known works, especially compared to his far-reaching novels *Men in the Sun* (1962) and *All That's Left for You* (1966), this short story is no less representative of Kanafani's masterful storytelling. It is also just as representative of the often subliminal, disjointed, and non-linear narrative style that he is known for and through which he vividly captures the harsh and unforgiving realities of refugee life and displacement in which countless Palestinians found themselves after 1948. "The Stolen Shirt" is the first story in a larger posthumous collection of Kanafani's short stories, *The Stolen Shirt and Other Stories*, which was first published in 1982 in Beirut, Lebanon, by *Mu'assasat al-'Abḥāth al-'Arabiyyah* (Institute of Arab Research). A second edition was published in 1987 by the same publisher.

The Stolen Shirt[1]

Holding back the blasphemous swearing that nearly slipped off his tongue, he raised his head to the dark sky. He could feel the black clouds gather like pieces of basalt, overlapping and then dissipating.

This rain will not stop tonight. This means that he will not sleep, but instead he'll stay hunched over his shovel, digging a path to divert the muddy water away from the tent poles. His back has become virtually impervious to the beating of the cold rain upon it. The cold gives him a pleasant feeling of numbness.

He smells the smoke. His wife has started a fire to bake the flour into bread. How he wants to be finished with this trench, to go inside the tent and shove his cold hands into the fire until they burn. If he could, he would just grab the flame with his fingers and move it from one hand to the other until the frost disappeared from both. But he's afraid to enter this tent. For in his wife's eyes there is a terrifying question that has been there a long time—and even the cold is less unforgiving than the terrible question. If he enters she will say to him, planting her palms into the dough and her eyes into his:

"Have you found work? . . . What will we eat then? . . . How was so-and-so able to get work here and how was so-and-so able to get work there?"

Then she will point to Abd Al-Rahman, curled up in the corner of the tent like a miserable wet cat, and shake her head in a silence harsher than a thousand reproaches. What'll he have to say to her tonight other than what he says every night:

"Do you want me to steal to solve Abd Al-Rahman's problems?"

He stood up straight in a second of panting silence, then hunched over the broken shovel again and began to stare at the dark tent, feeling a great panic as he asked himself:

"And what if I stole?"

The supply depots of the International Relief Agency are close to the tents, and if he decided to go through with it then he could surely sneak—by means of a hole in the wall he'd find here or

[1] This translation was initially published on the website *Jadaliyya*. It is republished in print by permission.

there—into where the flour and rice are piled up. The money there does not belong to anybody. It has come from over there, from people whom Abd Al-Rahman's school teacher said are hypocrites, who "kill the victim and march at his funeral."

What harm would it do anyone if he were to steal a bag of flour . . . two bags . . . ten? And what if he were to sell some of this flour to one of those people who have a great ability to sniff stolen goods and a greater ability to bargain their prices?

The idea became more appealing to him. So he pressed on with even stronger determination to finish digging the trench around the tent and began to ask himself again why he shouldn't get started with his scheme tonight. The rain is intense, and the guard is more concerned with the cold than the interests of the International Relief Agency. So why not start now? Why?

"What are you doing, Abu Al-Abd?"

He raised his head in the direction of the voice and made out the shadow of Abu Sameer approaching from the two rows of tents pitched endlessly across the darkness.

"I'm digging flour."

"You're digging what?"

"I'm digging . . . I'm digging a trench."

He heard Abu Sameer's thin laugh that quickly dissipated into his whispering:

"It seems you're thinking of flour. The rationing will be delayed until after the first ten days of next month, about fifteen days from now, so don't think about it now unless you intend to 'borrow' a bag or two from the depot."

He saw Abu Sameer's arm point toward the depots, and he made out the shadow of a perverse smile on his thick lips. He sensed the difficulty of the situation, so he resumed prodding the ground with his broken shovel.

"Take this cigarette . . . Oh wait—no—it won't do you any good in this rain. I forgot it was raining—I have flour for brains."

A feeling of suffocating irritation began to close in on him. He has hated Abu Sameer for a long time—this repulsive chatterbox.

"What brings you out in this rain?"

"I came out . . . I came out to see if you wanted help."

"No thanks . . ."

"Will you dig for a while?"

"Most of the night."

"Didn't I tell you to dig your trench during the day? You're always going who-knows-where and leaving camp . . . do you go looking for the Seal of Solomon?"

"No . . . for work . . ."

Panting, he raised his head from the shovel.

"Why don't you go to sleep and leave me alone?"

Abu Sameer drew nearer with an ominous silence. He placed his big hand on Abu Al-Abd's shoulder, shaking it slowly as he said in a raspy voice:

"Listen, Abu Al-Abd, if you see a bag of flour disappear before your eyes in a little while now, don't let word of it slip out to anyone."

"What?" Abu Al-Abd said, his heart beating violently. He smelled the stench of tobacco from Abu Sameer's mouth, who whispered with wide open eyes:

"There are bags of flour that leave at night and go over there."

"Over where?"

"Over there."

Abu Al-Abd tried to see where Abu Sameer was pointing, but he found the man's arms hanging at his sides and heard his voice whisper with a deep rasp:

"You'll get your cut."

"Is there a hole that you guys enter through?"

Curling his tongue coyly, Abu Sameer cocked his head upward in denial, then rasped with a whisper:

"The bags of flour leave all by themselves . . . they walk!"

"You're crazy."

"No, you're the unfortunate one . . . Listen. Let's get right down to business. What we have to do is get the bags of flour out of the depot and take them over there. The guard will prepare everything for us as he always does. The one who will see to the sale isn't me, and it's not you—it's the blond American at the agency . . . No, no, it'll be fine, everything will make sense after the agreement. The American sells and I profit . . . the guard profits . . . You profit . . . and it's all by our mutual agreement. So what d'ya say?"

Abu Al-Abd felt the issue far more complicated than stealing a bag, two, or ten of flour, and a feeling full of disgust came over him at the thought of dealing with this human being, obnoxious and insufferable like the whole camp had come to know him.

But at the same time he drew great comfort from the thought of being able to return to his tent one day with a new shirt for Abd Al-Rahman and some small provisions for his wife after this long spate of deprivation. How beautiful their two smiles would be. The chance to see Abd Al-Rahman's smile alone would undoubtedly merit going through with the proposed scheme.

But what if he failed? . . . What miserable fate would await his wife and son . . . that would be the day Abd Al-Rahman carries around a shoe-shining box to hunch over it in the streets, shaking his small head over the customers' fine shoes. Miserable fate be damned.

But if he succeeded, then Abd Al-Rahman would seem like a new person, and he would rid that terrifying question from his wife's eyes. If he succeeded, then the misery of the trench every rainy night would end, and he'd live somewhere he can't even imagine right now.

"Why don't you leave this damned trench so we can start before the sun rises?" Abu Sameer said.

Yes, why not leave the trench? Abd Al-Rahman is in the corner of the tent panting from the cold, and he can almost feel his son's breaths brushing across his own cold forehead. How he wishes he could save Abd Al-Rahman from his misery and emaciation.

The rain has almost ceased, and the moon has started to tear a rugged path in the sky.

And Abu Sameer still stands there in front of him like a black ghost, planting his two huge feet in the mud, raising the collar of his old coat above his ears, standing and waiting. This person standing in front of him, proffering with him a vague new fortune, entreating him to help remove the bags from the depot, to some place, where the American would come every month and stand in front of the piles of flour, rubbing his clean palms together while laughing with blue eyes like those of a cat waiting to pounce upon some poor unsuspecting mouse.

"Since when have you dealt with this guard and that employee?"

"Do you want to do this with me, or just take the price of the flour to go and bribe the bastards? Listen. The American is my friend, and he's a person who likes tidy work. He always asks me to prioritize time, and he doesn't like lateness to jobs. We have to start now. Hurry."

He again pictured the American standing in front of the flour bags, laughing with narrow blue eyes and rubbing his clean palms together in delight and self-assuredness, and he felt a strange agitation. It occurred to him that that American was selling the flour all the while telling the women and children of the camp that rations would be delayed until after the tenth day of the month. At this he felt a raging flood of resentment, itself the echo of his feelings one day when he had been returning from the depots to tell his wife in a broken voice that they postponed the flour distribution ten days. How painful was the letdown that was drawn across her toil-ridden brown face. He had felt a thousand-pound lump in his throat as she looked in terrifying silence at the empty flour sack swinging from his arm like a hangman from a noose. In that glance of hers she meant that ten days would pass before they came across any flour for food. It also seemed that Abd Al-Rahman fully understood the situation, for he had long ceased his incessant demands to be fed.

In every tent of the refugee camp, eager eyes were sinking with that very same letdown. Each child in the camp had to wait ten days just to eat bread.

This, then, is the cause of the delays—Abu Sameer—standing in front of him like a black ghost, planting his feet in the mud anxious over the outcome of his dealings, him and the American who rubs his clean palms together in front of the flour piles while laughing with narrow blue eyes.

He didn't know how he lifted the shovel high above his head, or how he smashed it with an awesome violence into Abu Sameer's head. Nor did he know how his wife managed to pull him away from Abu Sameer's body, as he screamed in her face that the flour distribution would not be delayed this month . . .

All that he knows is that when he finally found himself back in his tent, drenched in water and mud, he embraced his son Abd Al-Rahman as he looked into his yellow emaciated face . . .

He still wanted to see him smile at the sight of a new shirt . . .

So he began to cry . . .

Jan Dost

From *Safe Corridor*

Translated by Marilyn Booth

Translator's Reflection

In early 2019, the Turkish army and supporting military groups attacked the Afrin region of Syria, whose inhabitants are mostly Kurds. The army occupied the region and, as a result, Afrin's people fled.

Jan Dost, Syrian Kurdish author and published poet residing in Germany, has written several war-centered novels since the civil war began in his native country. *Safe Corridor* (2019) focuses on the violent occupation of Afrin. It is a companion novel to *A Green Bus Leaves Aleppo* (2019), a novel in which Dost recounts essentially the same story from a different character's perspective.

Safe Corridor draws attention to the terrible impacts of war, visible and invisible, on children. The protagonist and narrator, Kamiran, is a young boy about 13 years of age, who, as a result of the terrible war-like situation and painful family events, wets himself regularly at night. His father has been captured by Daesh/ISIS in Manbij, the village where they live. Then, his five-year-old sister is killed by a bomb. These traumatic events have left his mother mute—literally speechless. Kamiran's voice frames the narrative. Now unable to attend school, Kamiran tells the details of life in Manbij, Aleppo, and Afrin, the tragedies he has witnessed, the path of internal displacement. Who is his listener? A piece of commercial pale-yellow chalk, taken from his school, which he treasures and protects.

The novel begins with a surreal image: in his family's tent in the refugee camp, Kamiran himself slowly turns into a massive lump of chalk. His body and his organs harden, as he lies in bed, motionless under the coverlet. The excerpt here comprises the first chapter and most of the second chapter.

At first, the family—Kamiran, his mother, sister, and brother—flee from Manbij, heading to Aleppo. However, this city, too, becomes a war zone, and it is here that his sister was killed by a bomb. The reduced family leaves for Kamiran's uncle's house in Afrin. But there is no safety in Afrin either. Due to the Turkish offensive, they find themselves in a refugee camp with thousands of other people who have left their homes. Thus, quite matter-of-factly, Kamiran narrates the dramatic stages and hardships of their lives in Manbij, Aleppo, and Afrin and then in the refugee camp.

In Kamiran's narration, utterly gruesome images of war mirror his own transformation as they take on a surreal aspect (and yield macabre humor) through these accounts of people's lives in multiple displacements and migrations. Eventually, we see that the "safe corridor" the Turkish army allegedly opened for civilians is, in reality, not safe at all and is never sheltered as a "corridor" or an opportunity for "safe passage" (an alternative translation of the title) should be. For the refugees, it is akin to Golgotha for Christ, the place of his crucifixion according to Christian belief. It is a path that must be taken, a passage from one life to another that is inevitable but that offers no salvation.

The novel ends as it began. Kamiran, himself now inert chalk, is washed by the surge of a flood that begins to submerge the entire refugee camp. Kamiran cannot leave the bed to escape. His father's ghost appears and tells him to surrender to his fate. Kamiran slowly melts into the merciless flood, in an act of dismemberment. Chalk is an implement of writing, of telling, of memory, but in this tragic story, it is silent. It cannot survive. Erasure is not sufficient: it is destroyed. The will to remember is destroyed in the face of war, despite the momentary efforts of a child.

From *Safe Corridor*

Pale Chalk

On the evening when young Kamiran discovered that he was turning into a lump of chalk, the rain was bucketing down. The sound the drops splattering onto the tent walls made was exactly the same sound he had heard in Afrin—volleys of bullets, raining down two days before the town fell to occupation.

As he lay in bed, ready for sleep and just beginning to slide into its welcome sweetness, Kamiran sensed something odd going on, a change coming over his body. He felt his feet going rigid: that was the first sign of it. He had the sensation of losing his toes, as if they were bits of writing chalk breaking off and dropping with a thud onto the mattress. Almost immediately, he felt something similar, and equally peculiar, happening to his legs. They were stiffening, and they seemed to have fused together.

Slowly—deliciously—the sensation of it crept higher over his body. Thighs, buttocks, and then his prick, like another little segment of hard chalk. His belly, his chest. He felt the fingers of both hands plop heavily onto the mattress, although they didn't make a sound. He could make sense of what was happening only if he thought of it as a horrifically frightening nightmare—but, in fact, the boy felt no fear. He raised his head off the mattress—at least, as far as his neck would allow, since at that very moment, the stiffness had got as far as that. He was preoccupied, not unhappily, with observing these changes to his own body. Somehow, this transformation afforded an enjoyment greater, as far as he could remember, than any happiness he'd ever known. Yes, he was aware that it was out of the ordinary to feel such intense pleasure at this conversion of his flesh and skin into hard, calcified matter. The strongest emotion he felt was a fervent hope that what he was going through right now would not end. A longing that time would stop here, that he could hold onto these moments of gratification, grasp them with his fingers—even if his fingers had fallen off, like pieces of school chalk, to disappear into his bed.

In fact, matters had begun to take this strange course earlier, when they'd been on their voyage, he and his mother Layla, who never spoke now; his little brother, Alan; and his Uncle Ali, the *buzuq* player. To begin with, the four of them had left the town of Sharraan, not far from the Turkish border, fleeing the contingents of extremist militias who marched on the heels of the Turkish army. They took shelter with another brother of his mother's, Uncle Naasan, who lived in Afrin City and was quite a lot older. But then the units of the Turkish occupation force reached Afrin, and so they picked up and left again, in a great hurry, on the 17th of March 2018. At that time—before that time too—tens of thousands of civilians were in flight from the hellish Turkish bombardments. And they were just as afraid of the militias who had allied themselves with Turkey and were playing their part in the wholesale strafing of the entire Afrin region. And so it ended, in blood and fire—the era of self-rule that a Kurdish party in the north of Syria had proclaimed. For the Turks had seen that project as an immediate and existential threat to their national security which they could not allow to continue.

The earliest signs of Kamiran's metamorphosis—which would take less than a month to complete—appeared when they were stopped, near the military checkpoint outside the town of Kiimar, on the way to the famous Ziyara Crossing. The tractor pulling their wagon came to a dead stop. Kamiran and his family were packed into the cart along with some other refugees including a pregnant woman. Driving the tractor was Ali, whom everyone knew as Ali the *Buzuq* Player, Kamiran's uncle. It wasn't the roadblock that stopped them. Ali stopped because that poor, miserable woman went into labor suddenly just before they reached the Crossing. It was clear that she was in a lot of pain.

On that same day, Uncle Ali discovered that the skin on his nephew's neck was so desiccated that it was cracking. He didn't know anything about the disease called calcinosis cutis. It targets the layers of skin just below the body's surface, and various things can cause it, among them an excess of calcium in the blood. Young Kamiran did not give this any serious attention; it must be a simple ailment of sorts, to the point that he joked with his uncle as they stared at his scaly skin, "I'm afraid I'm turning into a fish."

Day by day, the patches of afflicted skin widened and length-ened. His fingers grew as stiff and dry as firewood. The skin on his legs, neck, back, and buttocks, and even his penis, dried out. What was truly odd was that despite the skin condition, he didn't feel any pain at all. For that reason, the camp's doctor, who worked for the Kurdish Red Crescent, didn't concern himself much. He just handed Kamiran some sedatives whose only effect was to rouse some bitter mockery, tossed back and forth between this concerned uncle and his sister's son.

By the time the dry-skin condition had more or less engulfed his entire body, Kamiran's yearning to write something had grown more pressing. But there was no proper place to write, and the surroundings were not hospitable. He began talking, instead, to his pale piece of chalk. He told her the things that had happened during these years of war, across its harsh months, its long days. He told her the secrets he had hid from his family. He gave vent to his feelings, and his fears, everything that was apt to fill the mind of a boy on the verge of his teens living through the terrors of an insane war in a country where reason had lost its ability to steer the course of anything or anyone.

Now, as this later stage of Kamiran's transformation drew to a close on this rainy night, his mother, forever silent, was asleep. He could hear her breathing and it comforted him. His brother, who had been in agony all day with the intense pains in his hands and chest caused by the burns he had sustained from the firing that morning, was turning over restlessly on his mattress, muttering and grunting. And meanwhile, his Uncle Ali, the young *buzuq* player, was sitting with his mates in a tent somewhere, some distance away, plucking his small lute and chatting the evening away as he usually did.

This night, the boy was alone with his ordeal, on his own with the astonishing changes making their way across his body; alone, too, with this harsh pleasure buffeting him, like gusts of cold wind hitting his skin from the tips of his toes to the parting on his scalp.

Kamiran wasn't thinking about what would happen in the next few moments—or about the fix he would be in when this small fam-ily discovered his condition. He didn't think about his mother, who would wake up the next morning and come to lift the blanket off him, ready to give his shoulder a shake as she always did, summoning him to breakfast. He did not think about his brother Alan, who might come and sit next to his head, pleading with him to undo the dressings over his burns and put new ones on, or letting him know that the burns weren't hurting so much now. He was not musing about his uncle either—Uncle Ali, who might come into the tent at any moment, cursing the camp and Turkey and the war and the Party, as he had been doing ever since he came to live in this ill-omened place.

Now he couldn't even see the ghostly shapes that had lived with him, a constant presence in his mind, before this operation took its course and turned him into a giant piece of chalk, 160 centimeters long. Inside him, so very much had changed. Now he belonged to a different world, one where time didn't matter—or at least, time didn't seem to be like any of the other forces of nature. At the end of the day, here he was, an inanimate object, a huge length of chalk inert beneath the heavy blanket, listening to the thud of raindrops that the storm hurled relentlessly against the matte-white outer skin of the tent.

Let Me Make the Introductions

My name is *Kaamiyran*. But you can just call me Kamiran. In fact, you ought to say my name that way, because it's really more accurate. In Kurdish, it means "the one who's blessed with luck."

My mother used to be an English teacher. Laila Aghazadeh is her name. My father—the surgeon, Dr. Farhad—was kidnapped by Daesh years ago, when we were still living in Manbij.

I don't think you know me very well, do you? Even though you have lived with me for two years now. I haven't written very many sentences with you. Not many at all, I'm afraid. Just a couple of shambolic slogans, I guess, like for instance, *Long live the Revolution*, or a saying like *al-Jaysh al-hurr Allah yahmiih*. God protect the Free Army. That's what I used to recite over and over along with my schoolmates at primary school in Manbij, before Daesh came. But I don't remember using you to write, for instance, *The people want the fall of the regime*. That was the sentence we kept on repeating, back when we were walking alongside the adults in their demonstrations. Or, there was the other one, *Your head will be eaten away . . .* and then one doesn't even need to say the rest: *Your head will be eaten away*, and that will make you as short and stubby as my little brother's penis. He hasn't been circumcised, my little brother.

I stole you one day—it was sometime in the autumn—I stole you from school. I thought you were so elegant. Slim, shiny, not like the other pieces of chalk, the cheap ones that came in white boxes with "Directorate of Education of Aleppo" stamped on them. Those "government" chalks were fat and stubby, and whenever you tried to write with them, they made a lot of chalk dust. And the lines they made were only faint ones. You'd try to write a word and one letter would appear clearly, but you could barely see the other letters, so the chalk mutilated the word you were trying to write. There was one of our teachers—he was taken by Daesh later on—one of our teachers who despised the chalk. He was so disgusted by that government chalk that he used to shout curses at it. One day, he was writing something on the board with one of these pieces of chalk, and then suddenly he threw it out the window. He said to us, coughing, "A revolution has started, and things have changed in this country, but the chalk has stayed the same. *You* have to start a revolution now, one that's going to bring down this god-awful chalk. Changing this chalk will certainly mean changing the regime which can't for the life of it produce sound chalk that doesn't kill people off!" *The people want the fall of the chalk*—

"Now, repeat after me: *The people want the fall of the chalk.*"

We yelled out this sentence until the chairs in the classroom were vibrating and all of us, all the pupils in the room, collapsed into laughter. The teacher slapped his hand against the table and ordered us to get quiet.

Laughter, yes, but it was a true disaster whenever the teacher ordered us to erase the chalkboard or when he wiped it clean himself. That white chalk dust filled the whole room. We always had to open the windows wide and air out the room, even if it was the middle of winter. The white chalk dust settled stubbornly on the teacher's hair and got into his eyebrows and mustache. He didn't look like a teacher anymore; he looked more like the miller in our town. He was always trying to brush the dust off his teacher clothes and shake it from his hair. All the while, he would be muttering to us, "I am going to die of asthma. This chalk causes asthma, it's worse than pollen and factory smoke. God's curses on the life of a teacher, before the revolution started, and on his life after it started too."

Yeah, that's exactly what was going on, my dear, pretty chalk, my elegant chalk. *That's* what the teachers' chalk was like, the chalk that the government makes in its factories. But you, my own piece of chalk, you'd come from somewhere else, somewhere outside the country! You were just lying there one day—on that day I stole you. Yeah, just lying there, still and silent, and you grabbed my attention, just by lying there at the edge of the green chalkboard. I shot my hand out, I was just playing, really! And then I hid you, very quickly but with a lot of care, I put you in my pocket, and I took you home. But even now, I still don't really understand why I did it. You were really appetizing, so tempting! Something, but I didn't know what it was, attracted me to you, pulled me. Maybe it's that I love to write, and I want to have *something* to say about everything that's going through my head. But then, after I took you, you changed, you were just a plain little piece of something tossed into a corner of my room which overlooked the main street in Manbij. Just a little piece of something that no one would think twice about, except for me. I heard you complaining, every day. It was as if you were actually talking to me. Like, as if you were saying, "Boy! Hey there! If you don't mean to write anything, why did you bring me home like this? C'mon, pick me up, and write something with me. Whatever you want to write. Just do it."

So things just went along like that until we were forced out of Manbij, and we headed for Aleppo—about two years ago I guess it was. We were on the point of leaving the house, I remember this, and suddenly something yanked me to you—again—it seemed like some mysterious force, I didn't know what it was, but I took you along with me. Once we were there—in Aleppo, I mean—I forgot about you completely. I think I forgot you because I didn't find a single wall there on which I could write any of the sentences or phrases that were whirling about in my head. The walls in the neighborhood where my grandpa lived, in Masakin Hanano, were either half-destroyed now, or they were already unsafe anyway, so fragile they were on the point of collapsing. Or they were walls nobody could come close to, because you would see warnings on them or nearby, left by some unidentified military authority. There was never any explanation to tell you why or how this wall was off-limits, or where the orders came from. Anyway, most of the time I was too afraid of going out into the street. A lot of kids were dying out there. One of them was my beautiful little sister, Maysoon. The children died of snipers and bombs, and they died crushed beneath the ruins of their collapsing houses. We saw it all during the time we lived in Aleppo.

When it started, we really did believe that anyone who was dying in the war must be army, or at least fighters of some sort. But then we discovered that the bombs and the missiles and the bullets—the damned sprays of bullets that were louder than a microphone when they got close—were one-hundred-percent blind.

Back when we were still living in Manbij, I always carried you around in my pocket. I was waiting for just the right opportunity to write out one of the things my father used to say. My father, the surgeon Farhad. Before Daesh snatched him and he disappeared from sight and no one ever saw him again. There was one sentence my father repeated a million times in my hearing, and it really affected me. I knew it by heart as well as I knew the first verse of the Quran.

"All revolutions are alike, Kamiran, my boy. They're just like ass droppings—you can't tell one from another. Or like hair—every one like its twin brother. *Baarra, shaarra!*"

I didn't understand what my father was getting at with this sentence of his, but I learned it word-for-word anyway. And then my father disappeared all of a sudden. We waited for him, we waited a long time. My mother waited for him. She began standing, every evening, at the window, with Maysoon. They would be peering out the window, ready to catch the very first glimpse of him, but it was never any use. Then my grandfather arranged to bring us surreptitiously to Aleppo. And from there, and after my little sister, Maysoon, was killed in the bombing, we fled again, to Afrin. Running from one place to another, I forgot about you, I kept forgetting about you. But even though you weren't inside my head, and I didn't write anything with you, I never left you alone, not for a single day. No, I took you with me wherever I went. I guess there must be some secret to it, the way I take care of you. You're like a witch, my ghostly piece of chalk. I think *you* have some secret that you haven't told me ever.

What I think is—I have to write my father's words of wisdom out somewhere. But where shall I write all of this? Across my own palm, or across the enormous behind of our neighbor, Mazyat?

Of course, you wouldn't know our neighbor Mazyat, my dear chalk. My pale, thin friend. No, of course not. How would a piece of chalk with no features to speak of and no feelings get to know a village widow with such miserable luck and so much sex appeal?

This Mazyat was our neighbor back in Sharraan, the town near the Turkish border where we used to live. I'm not going to tell you about her right now. It would just make your saliva run, and then I'm sure you would melt away. Yeah, you see, your saliva would come streaming out just as if you were a bitch in heat. Any talk of Mazyat and even the saliva of saints and pious men starts flowing.

Anyway, my girl, my thin little friend, this isn't the time or space for talking about Mazyat's behind, or the smell she gave off, which I'm sure would make heads swim even among those men on the other side of the border, the Turkish gendarmerie, I mean. I'll come back to it, this subject of Mazyat, when you and I are alone, and when my brother Alan isn't with us here, that little lice-shit who doesn't know how to keep a secret.

Maybe you are feeling really surprised that I'm even talking to you now, since two years ago, I didn't talk to you. Maybe you are saying to yourself, "This boy is talking nonsense. He must have smoked a wad of hash or found some white powder to sniff."

Believe me, I haven't sniffed anything except you, that smell which reminds me of the way the walls in our school smelled and the board in our classroom in the primary school in Manbij, which we fled. I haven't inhaled anything except the pale dust you make, waves of tiny particles on which I can float. You are right, my dear, to object to my silence, and my neglecting you, for two years now. And then, well, why am I talking to you now if I didn't then? Because I was so stupid then that I believed a piece of chalk has no feelings, and doesn't sense anything, that she can't have any kind of relationship with a human being. I didn't know you, and that's why I didn't introduce myself or say anything to you.

It's the war, my friend. The war taught me that everything can feel stuff. Even if it's the little bullet that bores into people's bones, it doesn't matter whether they are soldiers or ordinary people from town; still, that little bullet might be very sensitive—it might feel as much as the finger that presses down on the trigger feels as it frees the poor little bullet from its tiny cave in the muzzle. And also, just like the war taught me that everything has feelings, it also taught me that a person's most trivial possession, when they're in the midst of a war, is exactly this—their senses, their feelings. In fact, it's their feelings that are responsible for whatever agony and horror they go through.

Now I'm going to tell you a little secret. It's not really important, as secrets go, but I'm going to tell you it anyway. Think of it as a confession from a child who is scared of being punished. One day, I had the guts to poke a cheap thick pasty-white piece of chalk into the behind of the teacher's son. This was the teacher who arrived after the nice, funny teacher who cursed out the chalk wasn't there anymore. I hated this teacher's son; I hated him a whole lot. He used to swagger around in the school courtyard because his father, the new teacher, was related to one of the Daesh emirs. One day, when we were standing at the green chalkboard drawing tanks and helicopters, that boy started chanting at me: "Your dad was treating the men from the Free Army. Your father's one of the Sahawat."

"Sahawat?" I said it in a way that showed I didn't believe him. Anyway, it was the first time I'd heard that strange name. Sahawat! But even if I hadn't heard it before, I understood that this word was definitely meant as an insult. Then I learned that it meant someone who didn't bow their head to Daesh, or maybe even who didn't help them. I was furious.

"My dad, Sahawat? Well your mama's a whore." I had him by the collar. The other boys stared at us, worried but also curious. They were in their seats, sitting "properly"—that is, with their hands stuck under their armpits, the way they were supposed to sit whenever the teacher entered the classroom.

He was wearing a blue tracksuit. I put out my hands and yanked the bottoms down, exposing his brown behind, soft and fleshy and darker in the middle. The bastard swung around to stand with his back to the chalkboard, trying to protect his backside from the curious eyes of his classmates, darting looks at him like arrows. But I jerked him forward to my chest, and then, holding him, I turned and forced him to stand with his butt facing the class so all the students could see him like this. They clapped and began shouting and striking their hands against their chairs. Then they split up into two teams, one of them urging me on and the other one supporting him.

"I'm going to fuck your whole family's daftar."

I'd learned this insult from my Uncle Ali—after all, these government-issued identity booklets, recording marriages and children's names, were as precious as you could get. As I jeered at him, I was reaching for a piece of fat white government chalk, as thick and gross as the finger of a big fat man. It was at the edge of the board, exactly where you'd been lying before, and I had just had the wickedest idea.

"Give me one reason not to push this stupid second-rate chalk into your third-rate bum."

Author's acknowledgment:

My gratitude goes to all who have provided information that benefited me in writing this novel, especially my friend, Engineer Salah Hanan, of Afrin.

Haji Jabir

From *Fatima's Harbor*

Translated by Nancy Roberts

Translator's Reflection

I feel privileged to have had the opportunity to translate *Fatima's Harbor* by Haji Jabir, not only because the narrative swept me along from one page to the next, drawing me continuously into the struggles faced by its main character and those around him, but also because the novel introduces the reader to events and issues that have caused tremendous suffering to many in the author's homeland, yet without the world being properly aware of them. By translating it into English, I'm given the chance to present this important piece of writing to a wider audience.

Fatima's Harbor is one of the few works of fiction that have addressed the plight of Eritrean refugees or the issue of forced migration and displacement within and beyond Africa generally. Although its Arabic edition was published in 2013 (Beirut: Arab Cultural Center), many of the scenes in *Fatima's Harbor* remain tragically accurate reflections of situations and phenomena that persist to this day. According to the 2017–2018 Amnesty International Report on Eritrea, thousands of Eritreans fled the country during the time period covered by the report. Government authorities continue to impose severe restrictions on the right to leave the country while severe human rights violations are committed regularly against those seeking to flee.

The long-standing ordeal faced by Eritrean refugees is an outgrowth of the 30-year War of Independence waged by Eritrea against Ethiopia (1961–1991), coupled with a civil war in Ethiopia and a further outbreak of hostilities between the two governments between 1998 and 2000. The social injustices resulting from these conflicts are rife and deep-seated, especially given the exploitation of the cause of Eritrean liberation in the service of greed and corruption.

This excerpt depicts the plight of Eritreans fleeing to Sudan who are caught up in a nightmare of kidnapping, sexual assault, human trafficking, debt slavery, and an underground trade in illegal organs that leaves people maimed and sometimes dead. The following narrative depicts the disfigurement and enslavement of the human spirit that take place as a result of such practices, as well as the resiliency of that same spirit and the cyclical nature of human experience—or, put another way, human existence as suffering with threads of compassion, courage, joy, and hope woven in.

From *Fatima's Harbor*

(2)

I woke to excruciating pain in the back of my head. I ran my hand over the place where it hurt. It was moist. I tried to open my eyes, but the glare from the sun was too bright. After repeated attempts, I began to recognize my surroundings.

I was inside a huge steel shipping container with a partially open roof. Next to me lay a number of people, including some women. As I came to, I noticed that most of them were sick or in otherwise bad condition. I tried to get up, but I was too dizzy. My eyes darted back and forth between the door and the people around me. I glimpsed a girl who was staring at me, a frightened look in her eyes. I asked her what was going on, but she looked away and didn't answer.

"*Salaamaat! Salaamaat!* Hope you're feeling better!"

The voice of a man who had just burst into the shipping container aroused terror in those present. He was addressing me, his face plastered with a malevolent grin. Shocks of unkempt hair protruded from beneath his skewed turban, his clothes were tattered, and a Kalashnikov rifle dangled from his shoulder.

He instructed me to get up. When I told him I was in too much pain, he grabbed me by my shirt and pulled me roughly toward him, forcing me to stand up in spite of myself before thrusting me just as forcefully to the floor.

"*Goom, wa khallii 'annak al-dal'. Hallil nawmtak!*" he barked.[1]

I hadn't understood a word he said, and he didn't give me a chance to ask for clarification but stalked out in a hurry. When I looked over again at the people around me, fear was written all over their faces.

Before long I started hearing a commotion and mingled voices. Then a number of young men and women were brought in, their hands and feet bound, and the door slammed shut behind them. By this time the place was wall-to-wall people, forcing me to huddle where I sat.

But finally I had a chance to start figuring out what was going on.

---

[1] "Get up, and cut the spoiled brat act. Make yourself useful!"

One of them said, "We've been detained by the Shifta,[2] and they won't let us continue on to Sudan unless we pay up."

"Pay up? What do the Shifta have to do with your going to Sudan?" I asked.

The guy sitting next to me was about to answer my question when he was distracted by the sound of chains at the door. Two men came in, grabbed the sick girl next to me, and led her out amid her hysterical screams.

"Khadija's time ran out today. I knew as soon as you got here."

I shot the guy a questioning look.

"The Shifta give everybody a time limit to pay what they owe before they send them to Sinai, especially if they're sick. It generally happens when a new prisoner comes."

"And what about you? When will your time be up?"

As the commotion in the shipping container died down, Abraham started telling his story. He had fled from military service four months earlier, and the Shifta had agreed to deliver him to Sudan for 3,000 dollars. He'd managed to pay half of it in advance by selling his mother's gold, but he hadn't been able to come up with the other half. And Abraham's troubles hadn't stopped there. As soon as the authorities in Asmara learned of his escape, they jailed his sick mother as a way of pressuring him to come back, saying that unless he did, she would have to pay 50,000 nafkas in return for her release.

Abraham teared up as he talked about the irony in the fact that in essence, both he and his mother were being held for ransom—he by a gang, and she by the State.

"The government awarded my mother 5,000 nakfas when my brother was martyred after volunteering to go to war, and here they are demanding that she pay 50,000 nakfas to punish us for my not wanting to join the army!"

He told me what he'd been through at Sawa, which was what had driven him to run away. Listening to Abraham was like hearing

---

[2] Translator's note: The term *shiftā*, used in Eritrea and some parts of Sudan, means "gang" or "highway robbers."

the same story for the hundredth time, so often had I experienced the very same things. And it was no different when he got to the part about what he'd been through with the Shifta.

"We're forced to gather firewood, graze the livestock, and clean the Shifta's cars in return for our food. But I'm trying to work extra hours so that I can reduce the amount I owe."

Listening to Abraham, another irony became apparent to me as I recalled what Kaddani had said about the way the Eritrean government put university students to work in return for food.

Abraham started talking again, so I turned my attention back to him.

I asked him about some of the sick women and elderly. Pointing to one corner of the shipping container, he replied, "That woman may be the next one to be taken away after Khadija. She still hasn't found anybody to pay the rest of the money she owes. As for the kids, God knows what'll happen to them. Most of them get smuggled to Sinai."

The word "Sinai" kept coming up as Abraham talked. I wanted to ask him about it, but our conversation was interrupted when a Shiftai came in. He gestured to me, so I got up and followed him out. We went into a small tent where there was a group of men surrounded by a collection of Kalashnikovs and cell phones. A woman was preparing coffee for them, while two others were busy cleaning the tent and washing clothes.

"You've got a week to come up with 25,000 nakfas, or else we'll come up with some arrangement of our own for you. Until then, you've got to work and make yourself useful."

Replying to the one who appeared to be the leader, I said, "I never made any agreement with you all to be taken to Sudan in the first place. You took my car, kidnapped me, and brought me here against my will."

He just laughed and was joined by the others.

"Well, now that you're here, you're here, like it or not!"

I remembered my mother, who had always warned me, "Never trust a Shiftai, even if he's your brother. Treachery runs in their blood. It's enough to know that during the revolution,[3] they used to steal the rebels' weapons, then sell them back to them."

I used to come in contact with them while I was pasturing live-stock in the open areas around Ghinda, and we would have brief exchanges. But if I asked them what village they were from, I never got any answer. And I was always amazed at their coarse way of talking. So I asked my mother about them, and she told me they'd come to Eritrea recently from some distant desert, which helped to explain why their speech, their manners, and their way of dressing were so different from ours. People had called them various names at first, but the one that stuck was "highway robbers," so much so that the term came to be understood automatically to refer to them.

When I got back to the shipping container, I told Abraham what had happened with me.

"Welcome, friend, to the Shifta State!" he replied with bitter sarcasm.

(3)

The next morning, I was assigned the task of transferring piles of firewood from the back of a large truck to a storage tent. It was hard for me to lift even a single bundle, but I wasn't allowed to rest. An armed Shiftai stood some distance away watching me and others, and he would punish anybody who stopped working by doubling his duties.

At noon we got our first break. I felt a lifetime of weariness sweeping over me. Together with other workers exhausted from their various tasks, I came straggling back into the shipping container, where we were awaited by dry bread and lentils. I was ravenous, but I made a point of eating really slowly, hoping to gain as much time as I could away from the misery of the firewood. I wasn't alone, as it was obvious that everybody was resorting to the same trick.

I looked around in search of Abraham, but he hadn't come yet. The time flew by, and before I knew it, the Shiftai was ordering us

---

[3] Translator's note: A reference to the Eritrean War of Independence, fought between September 1, 1961, and May 24, 1991, for autonomy from Ethiopia.

back to work. When I reached the work site, I found two additional trucks parked next to the one I hadn't finished yet. My taskmaster told me I would have to finish all three truckloads by sundown. He was obviously trying to get a rise out of me, so I thought it best to make no objection.

By sunset, I had nearly finished all three truckloads, but I couldn't feel my hands anymore, and my back hurt so much I was nearly doubled over from the pain. I asked the Shiftai to let me put off what was left till the next morning, but he rejected the request out of hand, so I was forced to keep going.

I came back to the shipping container in shackles, dragging my feet from sheer exhaustion, and collapsed into an empty corner. It wasn't until quite some time later that Abraham came in. He looked dog-tired, and I was shocked to see his feet covered with bloody wounds. Stretching out beside me, he asked how my first day had gone, so I told him what had happened with me. When I asked him about his day, he told me he'd been working nonstop since morning to shrink the debt he owed. He hadn't even eaten.

"It's best," he said. "This way I can shorten my time here."

I felt sorry for Abraham. I ran my fingers over the inner pocket where I kept the money Jibril had given me together with what I'd saved up during my time working for Hajj Burhan. I wished I could put an end to his suffering and mine by paying what we both owed the Shifta. Then we could leave for Sudan together.

Interrupting my train of thought, Abraham said, "Don't worry about me. As long as I'm useful to the Shifta, I can at least protect myself from their trickery. After being here so long, I've gotten to know what makes them tick. Actually, I knew a lot about them before I got here."

What he'd said piqued my curiosity. I asked him to tell me more about them.

"The Shifta—'the Gang'—are nomadic Bedouin who came to Sudan after their territories were hit by drought. Then the sharifs, or nobility, joined forces against them and drove them off their lands. They lived in Sudan for a period of time until the Mahdist Revolt that began in 1881. When the Mahdists waged war on them, the Shifta sought refuge in Eritrea, where they established friendly relations with the Italians. But most of them went back to Sudan as soon as the Mahdi was defeated and his revolt had been put down."

"I didn't see any of them at Sawa."

"The Shifta have Sudanese citizenship, and they take advantage of it to get out of military service in Eritrea, just as they use their Eritrean citizenship to weasel out of any responsibilities in Sudan. This has made it easy for them to move back and forth across the Sudanese-Eritrean border. Did you know that they have satellite phones and four-wheel drive trucks and jeeps? And it's all been made possible by smuggling operations."

"Human smuggling, you mean?"

"Yeah. Some of them work smuggling people into Sudan, and business is booming, as you can see. But others smuggle arms and other merchandise in and out of the country, and they enjoy protection from influential generals."

Our conversation was interrupted when the shipping container door opened again. A Shiftai stuck his head inside and pointed to a girl sitting in another corner. Without saying a word or making any objection, she got up and followed him, her eyes glued to the floor.

"That's Zainab. The Shifta rape her in return for reducing the debt she owes. We haven't been able to do anything. Somebody tried to object at first and they shot him dead."

What Abraham had just told me left me stunned. My blood boiling, I got up from where I sat, my fatigue suddenly giving way to a world-shattering rage. Abraham grabbed my hand, begging me not to doom myself to destruction.

"You won't do Zainab any good by getting yourself killed. If I had 1,000 dollars, which is all she has left of a 3,000 dollar debt, I would have helped her get out a long time ago. I've offered to double the work I do for them in return for their letting her go, but they refuse."

I had no idea that the Shifta were demanding that much from anybody. I felt paralyzed with helplessness. I could see now how hard it would be to free even myself. And to think I'd been fantasizing about taking Abraham with me! My breathing grew calmer, but my mind kept going in circles. I'd started weighing my own need for money against Zainab's and Abraham's, and I hated myself for it. It was obvious how terribly they were suffering. But at the same time, I felt overwhelmed by my own pain.

Sensing my inner struggle, Abraham started trying to make me feel better.

"Don't worry," he said. "There's not much left. Zainab will get out soon, and so will I. All I've got left to pay now is 500 dollars."

I was gripped by indecision all over again, only this time, it was fiercer than ever. What I had, although it wasn't enough to buy my own freedom, would be enough to liberate Zainab and Abraham. I debated over whether to work for the Shifta for a while until I could pay what I owed, or do what it took right then and there to ensure the release of the other two. What finally settled the matter for me was the sight of a broken Zainab trudging meekly toward her torture chamber.

Suddenly I got up and headed for the door. I knocked on it as hard as I could until a Shiftai came. I told him I needed to see his commander about an important matter. He shut the door in my face, but after a while he came back, let me out, and escorted me to a nearby tent.

The minute I was allowed in to see their commander, I announced, "I want to pay."

He guffawed, "If only a fraction of them were like you and only took a day to cough up the cash!"

The commander called one of his subordinates and instructed him to get the car ready to take me to the border at dawn. As the man came toward me to release me from my shackles, I said quickly, "I'm paying for Zainab and Abraham."

Abraham and the others were surprised to see me coming back to the tent accompanied by Zainab, no longer in shackles. Even before I'd had a chance to sit down, he started raining me with questions.

"Oh," I said evasively. "I found a way to get her out. And not just for tonight—forever. I found a way to get you out too."

Abraham sat staring at me, waiting for me to explain the last thing I'd said.

All I added was, "Tomorrow the two of you will be driven to the Sudanese border. You'll finally have the chance to get your mother out of jail and start a new life."

Abraham tried repeatedly to figure out how I'd managed to win his release, but I succeeded in avoiding his many questions. I was starting to get drowsy, but I noticed Zainab coming over to me.

"Thank you," she said. "I'll never forget what you did for me, and I hope I can repay you some day."

Wanting to alleviate her sense of indebtedness toward me, I urged her to take care of herself and not to let anybody hurt her or take advantage of her ever again. But then I remembered something that she could do for me in return. I hesitated to say what it was, since my preoccupation seemed so trivial now by comparison with all Zainab had endured in this hellhole. But in the end, her inquisitive glances weighted the scales in favor of my heart's desire. So, despite my embarrassment and reservations, I asked her to look for Salma on her way home and to tell her that I loved her and had never forgotten her. Then I launched into my usual description of her:

"Salma's on the tall side," I said. "She's got a smooth, dark complexion, thick black hair, and a little mole along the edge of her upper lip. She also has an adorable speech impediment, as she can't say the 'r' quite right. Her hands . . ."

My voice trailed off as I engrossed myself in the sight of Salma in my mind's eye.

Her hands are the hearth that welcomes me home in an unwelcoming world, and in her arms, wishes turn to dreams that don't know the meaning of impossible. Out of her pristine smile flow springs of delight. Her presence . . .

Abraham was approaching, so, coming out of my poetic reverie, I changed the subject, telling Zainab and Abraham to prepare themselves for a new life. Then we all went to sleep.

Early the next morning, I slipped half the money I had left into their hands and said goodbye. Zainab tried to thank me again, but I cut her off, and she promised to look for Salma. The two of them got into a Land Rover that sped away with them down a sandy road before vanishing from sight. I thought back on the car that had fired at me and blown out my tire. So, then: it must have been a smuggling operation like the one that had just taken off with Zainab and Abraham.

I was jolted out of my reverie by the voice of the Shiftai as he ordered me to start working. I was heading for the firewood truck when he yelled, "Come away from there! You're going to take your brother's place now!"

My previous job had been a picnic compared to what faced me now. After transferring the shackles from my wrists to my feet, the Shiftai handed me a large ax. From where he stood, he pointed to a tree. As I made my way over to it, the protrusions on the iron shackles rubbed harshly against my skin with every step I took. Despite the weight of the ax, he wouldn't allow me to put it down even for a second. I asked him to take the shackles off my ankles so that I could move freely, but he wouldn't do it, justifying his refusal by saying I might try to attack him with the ax. I felt more than ever for Abraham and what he'd gone through cutting down trees all day.

I brought the ax down on the tree trunk with all the strength I could muster, but it wouldn't budge. I made a second try, and a third, as the Shiftai shrieked at me to swing harder. With every blow, more strength seeped out of me until I fell to the ground in exhaustion. The Shiftai started to come over to me, screaming again. Rising heavily to my feet, I took hold of the ax and tried to lift it but couldn't. I tried again, but it fell out of my hand, and I fell on top of it, splitting my head open. Panicking at the sight of my bloodied face, the Shiftai carried me to the truck and had me taken back to the shipping container. I walked in with a bandaged head and bleeding feet. Before closing the door, the Shiftai growled, "Watch your step. Or else, Sinai's waiting for you."

Once again I had the name "Sinai" ringing in my ears but without understanding what it meant. I closed my eyes and fell fast asleep.

No one demanded any work from me for the rest of that day, and by the following day, I'd started to recover my strength. At around noon, the Shiftai who had taken Zainab and Abraham to the Sudanese border came back to the shipping container. With a crafty smile on his face, he took me aside and handed me a piece of paper.

"The brother you did a favor for has done a favor for you this time!"

The paper was from Abraham. It said,

I've chosen the quickest way to ensure my mother's release and to reward you for what you did for me. After Zainab told me everything that happened, the only solution I could see was to have the Shiftai turn me over to the Eritrean border guard. He gets a hefty reward that he can split with you, and with that you can buy your own freedom. All I ask is that you keep this a secret from the rest of his gang. This way, my mother can go home. As for me, I'll deal with my own fate. Don't worry about me. The time I spent in the Shifta State toughened me up.

The letter distressed me on two accounts: first, on account of the lifetime Abraham had spent being tormented by the Shifta and, second, on account of the fact that even this torment hadn't led to his deliverance.

And when the gang member came back to talk to me again, he made things even worse:

"Tell me," he said. "I hope this letter is worth it. The poor guy nearly died to get it to you."

The Shiftai handed me the money, stressing the importance of keeping the deal a secret between us. When I asked him why he'd kept his promise to Abraham and betrayed his friends, he shocked me by saying that it had nothing to do with keeping promises but rather with making a profit. In other words, honesty is necessary in order to preserve the trust required to keep certain crimes going, since otherwise everything will collapse.

"So," I asked him, "if bounty hunting would be more profitable, then why don't you all work in that business instead?"

"Oh," he said. "We don't trust the government. They might sell us out without a moment's notice, whereas runaway soldiers can't do anything to us!

"Anyway," he went on, "get ready. You'll want to set out for Sudan as soon as the sun goes down."

The minute I paid what I owed, the Shifta commander ordered my shackles removed without asking me where the money had come from. Now I understood better what the Shiftai who'd delivered the letter meant by what he said about the importance of keeping commitments: it's the only way to ensure the continuation of crimes more heinous than broken promises.

As the sun set and I got into the car, I cast a final glance at the shipping container bursting at the seams with the ailing and oppressed. I wished I could save them all or, at the very least, ease their suffering, open a pinhole of hope and light onto their painful present. I wished what I had seen were nothing but a nightmare that would dissipate with the first rays of dawn. And I went on wishing until the car began rolling toward the Sudanese border. The shipping container with its tormented occupants receded farther and farther into the distance until the Shifta State disappeared entirely from view.

(4)

The vehicle turned off the road into a thickly wooded area. A short distance later, we came to another Shifta encampment consisting of a large shipping container and, next to it, a small tent. It looked so much like the place we'd been in before, at first I thought we'd gone back to where we'd come from. We were joined by four exhausted-looking people who took seats in the rear, and the vehicle headed back for the sandy road. I wanted to ask the driver about the place where we'd just stopped, but it was easy to see that it was another of the Shifta's improvised jails.

"If we get separated, everybody go back to the last place we were all together."

The driver's instructions put a smile on my face. They brought back memories of when Salma had told me about her school Girl Scout troop.

Today our team beat the other team, but just barely, and that was thanks to me! I remembered an important scout rule that says that if the team members get separated for any reason, they should go back to the last point where they were all together. This is what enabled us to win just when we were about to lose!

The only thing there to dispel the darkness of the night and my nonstop thoughts was the driver's loud voice as he made phone calls asking whether the road was safe. I understood some of what he said, but most of it went past me.

Whenever I asked him how long it would be before we got to Sudan, I got the same one-word reply: "*Shway* . . . in a little bit."

Leaning over toward him so the others wouldn't hear me, I asked him if he'd ever transported a girl by the name of Salma.

Looking at me in surprise, he replied matter-of-factly that he'd never been interested in knowing the name of anybody he'd transported.

Straightening up in my seat and peering into the dark void before me, I started describing her: "Salma's on the tall side," I said. "She's got a smooth, dark complexion, thick black hair, and a little mole along the edge of her upper lip. She also has an adorable speech impediment, as she can't say the 'r' quite right. Her presence . . ."

I stared through the windshield into the distance, summoning Salma's radiance in the midst of my darkness. No longer speaking to the Shiftai, I continued. "There's a glow to her presence that lends a special hue to both time and place, turning our moments into a memory that even years would be hard-pressed to erase. When she's with me, all else—however magical or brilliant—pales into nothingness."

The driver slowed down, his features registering what appeared at first to be a dull non-comprehension. But then suddenly he laughed out loud and, turning to me, exclaimed, "Well, if a girl like that got in my truck, I'd forget my own name, and I'd never let her go!"

Once again the driver veered onto a side road, at the end of which appeared a dim light that grew gradually brighter as we got closer to it until at last its source came into view: a number of four-wheel drive vehicles encircling a fire that would periodically flare as someone threw a log or branch into its flaming belly. Our vehicle joined the circle of fire and, after turning off the engine, the driver got out with a sword in his hand. In this he was followed by the drivers of the other vehicles which, I noted, bore Saudi and Kuwaiti license plates. A guy sitting next to me explained that the cars had been smuggled into the country.

Ams al-masaa . . . ghaabat al-shams.

Yesterday evening . . . the sun went down.

Ams al-masaa . . . ghaabat al-shams.

Yesterday evening . . . the sun went down.

The gang members divided themselves into two groups facing each other, one on either side of the fire, clapping and repeating the same phrase in song:

Ams al-masaa . . . ghaabat al-shams.

Yesterday evening . . . the sun went down.

Positioned between the two groups, a gang member danced nimbly with his sword. Facing one of the two groups, he moved the sword gracefully through the air, and its members began singing with greater gusto. Then he turned to the other group, and the same interaction ensued. The scene seemed to be building up to a climax. The more intense the sword-bearer's movements, the more enthusiastic the singers around him grew.

Ams al-masaa . . . ghaabat al-shams.

Yesterday evening . . . the sun went down.

I wondered why they would go on repeating a single phrase the entire time. It was likewise a mystery to me how they could enjoy dancing and singing in the middle of what, to me at least, was nothing but a dark, scary night. Even so, I and those with me were transfixed by the euphoric state that had come over the gathering. I also noticed that the refrain was divided between the two groups. It would begin with one group and end with the other as if in a never-ending counterpoint.

The driver came back drenched in perspiration, his enduring state of rapture plainly visible on his features. We passengers had climbed on top of the vehicle to get a good view of the scene, so he gestured us back to our places. The circle of vehicles had broken up by now, but that had done nothing to dampen his spirits: *Ams al-masaa . . . ghaabat al-shams.*

Looking back at us as he sang, the driver began gesturing with his hand. We didn't understand at first what he was asking us to do. But then he interrupted his singing long enough to say quickly: "Come on now, sing along with me: *Ams al-masaa . . . ghaabat al-shams.*"

We started repeating it with him, but our inability to keep up to his liking soured his mood.

"Never mind! Shut up now, you goddamned slaves."

There ensued an awkward silence, which I broke by asking him whether he considered himself an Eritrean. He gave me a disconcerted look before replying with a laugh, "Yes . . ."

"So," I asked, "Why would you refer to us as 'slaves' if you consider yourself one of us?"

He got a more serious look on his face. "Are you upset? Don't be. I didn't mean to insult you. That's the only name we've had for you for as long as I can remember. What do you want me to call you?"

Not in the mood to go on with the conversation, I looked away into the lightless expanse. Then suddenly another question came to mind. I asked him where he was from originally and whether he ever visited home.

"Where?" he said. "Home? From the time my ancestors had to leave it, nobody's been able to go back."

The Shiftai went on talking about Eritrea and how it had been a place of refuge for his ancestors when they'd been fleeing for their lives. He spoke about the country with such affection and gratitude that I felt confused, and I finally came to the conclusion that he couldn't see the inconsistency between this love and gratitude and the things he was doing. On the contrary, he seemed entirely at peace with his way of life, as though he'd never known anything else. For a moment there, I actually felt sorry for him. It occurred to me that the Shiftai and his victim were only separated by the most illusory of lines and that, in one way or another, the Shifta were victims themselves.

Getting back on his phone, the Shiftai slowed down and started looking left and right until he came to a full stop. All of us had started glancing around nervously when suddenly another Shiftai appeared, drawing a camel behind him. The two men stepped aside for a time, after which the driver came back and ordered us out of the vehicle.

"Come on now, you," he said. "You'll go the rest of the way with my brother here."

Nobody had the energy to argue with him. The Shiftai got into his vehicle and headed back to where he'd come from. We started looking back and forth at each other and at the new Shiftai, who was busy sorting some heavy ropes. After attaching the ropes to the camel's gear, he mounted the animal and ordered us to hold onto the ropes.

The camel took off, and we followed it on foot, clutching the ropes that dangled from it on either side as the Shiftai alternately sped up and slowed down. Eventually we came to an area which he told us was the last point where the Eritrean border guard was stationed.

I noticed search lights scanning the area, turning every dark spot into day. Dismounting quickly, the Shiftai knelt his camel and told us to get down. We stayed this way until the searchlights had passed. When he got up again, he shouted for us to run as fast as we could. Then, as soon as the searchlights came back in our direction, he went prostrate again. We kept on alternately running and going down on our bellies, our panting nearly rending the veil of the surrounding darkness. Even the camel seemed to have been trained to move instinctively away from the light, as it would halt of its own accord the minute it began approaching.

Once we were out of the searchlight's range, the Shiftai stopped and pointed to a road at the end of which there was another point of light.

"That's where you want to go," he said. "Once you've gotten there, you'll be in Sudan."

No sooner had the man finished speaking than we took off as fast as our legs would carry us. We were all fighting off our fatigue, giving this last leg of the journey everything we had. Sudan was getting closer and, with it, our most cherished hopes. I could see Salma in the point of light before me. She was smiling, waiting to put an end to the exhaustion of the days I'd endured without her, ready to wash away the agony of suspense, to refill my spirit drained dry by despair.

When I saw Salma, I knew my barren days without her were over, or nearly so. She poured down on me like rain, and everything within me turned green and succulent.

Spurred on by her beaming countenance, I got ahead of everybody else. Their panting was getting louder and louder, but they were no less determined than I was. I imagined what their wishes might be at this watershed moment. I imagined what the point of light meant to each one of them given the suffering that had been etched deep in their spirits.

There was a troubling moment when suddenly I thought about the fact that our salvation now lay in turning our backs to the homeland, in fleeing from it filled with a chaotic mishmash of fear and hope, doubt and certainty. It reminded me of something Kaddani had said: "The 'homeland' is a white lie that some promote without feeling guilty and which others latch onto without feeling duped."

As Sudan drew nearer, Eritrea began slipping away. After all, homelands are selfish: Neither of them would come around unless the other one left.

I can say with certainty of those who were running alongside me that as badly as they wanted to escape from their homeland, this very escape also caused them pain, and that as intent as they were on finding a life outside their own country, it would have terrified them for this country to die within them or for it to slip out through their ribs unnoticed before they'd been able to tuck it into the last hidden recesses of their souls.

I can say with certainty that these people were leaving Eritrea with disappointment seared indelibly on their brows, like church bells that, hardly having ceased to ring, announce themselves anew.

I can say with certainty that any country that no longer has room for its own people will find plenty of room for suffering and pain.

I can say with certainty that at that critical moment, they dreaded the possibility that as they crossed over into Sudan, they would be riddled with memories of childhoods spent on backstreets, grandmothers' coffee, and story-filled evenings.

I can say with certainty that there was nothing they feared more than their memory. Or rather, that they both feared it and feared for it, for now it had become their last line of defense in an unequal battle.

We ran with all our might while doing our best to avoid the broom bushes the villagers had planted as food for their livestock and as buffers against the sand dunes that encroached on their villages. As we fled, I thought about how badly we need "broom bushes" of another kind to prevent us from encroaching on each other's homelands, to act as buffers that can preserve our hopes, our dreams, and even our memories from ruin.

By now we were so close to the light that we couldn't see anything beyond it. A voice ordered us to kneel and place our hands on top of our heads. A man came up to us, brandishing a rifle in our faces. He was followed by others who bound us and searched us, then escorted us to the room of an officer who asked us why we had crossed the border. He grilled us on our military divisions and the weapons we'd been trained to use. Then he issued instructions for us to be taken to a prison that was bursting at the seams with fugitive Eritreans.

We were in the Sudanese border guard jail for several days. Every day we were packed in tighter than we had been the day before. Not an hour passed without a new group arriving, the weariness of a lifetime etched on their features.

Then deliverance came at last.

One morning, soldiers started taking us out in groups. When my turn came, I was brought again before the officer, who fingerprinted me, took a photo of me, and affixed it to my file, which I noticed had a number on it. Then he handed me a piece of paper that read "S-257307."

Poems by Gulala Nouri

Translated by Ali Harb

Translator's Reflection

There is an omnipresent melancholy in the poetry of Gulala Nouri. In her writings, there is a search for a home away from the homeland that always comes up short, rendering her a perpetual stranger. The poet does not revel in that state. On the contrary, Nouri seeks belonging.

The Iraqi poet observes those who live around her who are unburdened by the suffering of estrangement and the trauma of war. Life for them is a "straight line," she writes, drawing a contrast with her own tumultuous experiences. Those differences highlight the tensions between the poet in the diaspora and her immediate surroundings.

Nouri's poetry is deeply personal, but that struggle to rid oneself of the agony of being an outsider is not uncommon among immigrants. The human condition she describes is universal despite the uniqueness of her own experiences. Even though sadness is prevalent in her poetry, her writings do not reflect self-pity. She is defiant, almost rebellious. She questions the pain, but as she notes in one of the poems translated below, pain needs no excuse to be present sometimes.

No Flowers On My Doorstep

My home sits on the corner of an intersection
like the final corner of my life,
small and divergent.
I leave the door open often,
for I have no jewelry to fear for

And on my doorstep, I place no potted plants.
Flowers are not for me,
I tell the wooden ladder.
They are for the women who engineer
the width of the lines of their marriages
and the length of their secret affairs

They are not for me.
Flowers are a quiet anxiety linked to precise thinking about water
and I am a multitude of oceans catching a torrent of tears
coming from every direction

Doorstep flowers are delicate and pampered
but I am a forest who doesn't tire of intense staring.
I promenade with the reptiles
and dine on meteors of dead friends' souls

Flowers are not for me.
I've been bereaved many times
when people have plucked them from me—
sometimes for departing soldiers,
and other times for soldiers returning in caskets.
There, my flowers are orphaned of light
and I am orphaned here in this house on the intersection

On the opposite corner,
my neighbor, who has baskets of flowers on her doorstep,
has never known war.
She draws a straight line to define life
while I define war as a series of near misses and survivals

لا زهور على عتبة بيتي

يقع بيتي في ركن تقاطع طرق
مثل الركن الأخير لعمري،
صغير ومتشعب.
أترك الباب مفتوحاً غالباً
فلا جواهر أخاف عليها
وعلى العتبة لا أضع الأصيص
الزهور ليست لي
أقول للسُلّم الخشبي ..
إنها للنساء المهندسات لخطوط عرض الزواج
وطول علاقاتهنّ السريّة.
إنها ليست لي
الزهور قلق هادئ يتعلق بتفكيرٍ دقيقٍ حول الماء،
وأنا محيطات لفوضى دمعٍ في الجهات كلها.
زهور العتبات رقيقات ومغنجات
وأنا غابة من تحديقٍ حادٍ لا أنعس،
أتنزه مع الزواحف
وأتعشى شهاباً من أرواح أصدقاءٍ موتى،
الزهور ليست لي،
لقد ثُكلت مرات
وهم يقطفونها مني
تارةً من أجل جنود يغادرون
وأخرى لِجنود عائدين في تابوت.
زهوري هناك يتيمة من ضوء
وأنا يتيمة هنا في بيت على تقاطع طرق
في ركنه المقابل
جارتي التي في عتبة بابها سلال الزهور،
التي لا تعرف الحرب
وتعرّف الحياة بخط مستقيم.
بينما أعرّف الحرب كثيمة لنجاةٍ ما.

Like an Oak Leaf

In the vacant streets of Dearborn,
I fall like an oak leaf,
like a child with no playmate
except the cold wind of February's ice

It takes me in all directions
It blows me away lightly for a time, tumbling me under luxury cars,
then hurls me onto the quiet homes
of families watching funny movies,
or sitting gleefully around a meal

I have no aim as a leaf except the abyss
My limbs get worn out from moving in all directions
and I crumble . . .
Some of me settles in the corner of a knafeh shop,
other bits at the Dollar Tree store,
while another part gets singed by a cigarette carelessly tossed by an
    addict

As for my core, it gets stuck in the gutter of a dead city,
overlooking heads that seem never to have left their place

كورقة لِشجرة سنديان

في الشوارع الفارغة لديربورن
أسقط مثل ورقة لِشجرة سنديان
كطفلة لا شريك لها
غير ريح باردة لَثلج شباط
تأخذني لكل الاتجاهات
تطيرني خفيفة حيناً.. تُدحرِجني تحت سياراتٍ فارهةٍ
تقذفني على البيوت الساكنة
لعوائل تشاهد فيلماً كوميدياً
أو تجتمع بمرح على المائدة.
لا هدف لي كورقة تسقط سوى الهاوية
تتآكل أطرافي من تنقلي بين الاتجاهات
وأتَفتت..
بعضي يستقر في ركن لمحل كنافة
وبعضي الآخر في محل (دولار تري)
وجزء مني تحرقه سيجارة رماها مدمن بإهمال
أمّا نصلي فتعلق في مزراب مدينة ميتة
لرؤوس كأنها لم تغادر مواقعها أبدا.

Dissecting Pain—My Will for the Washer of the Dead[1]

Bind my corpse tightly
Put a lot of musk on it
so I don't smell your dead bodies
lying all around me

Stop the angels from accompanying me
so they don't steal the papers of my life,
the way my poems did,
and so I can curse liberally
without a wag of their wings

Don't wash my lips, please
Those kisses, in which I never lied, are my treasure
And don't praise your god when I smile
That's just me poking fun at this ablution
For my sins are many
Bury them with me
They'll be my only company when I am sent back as a stranger
as I always have been here

I love my unruly knees
Leave them this way
And do not braid my long hair
I love it just like this—disheveled, angry

I don't want to bid farewell to the house
where I died dozens of times
I won't miss a single corner of it
Spare your efforts
Let my final day among you pass without trouble
and repeat my name—from now on I am no longer a funeral

---

[1] This poem refers to rituals of preparing the dead for burial in accordance with Islamic tradition.

And please, I do not like the common white
Let my shroud be red
I have an adequate bundle of red lines that I crossed
Place all of them on my chest
These are my children who birthed me again and again

And lay me on my left side at last
unto an eternity
very close to my heart

تشريح الألم - وصيتي إلى مغسلة الموتى[2]

كمّمي جثتي بقوة

ضعي عليها الكثير من المسك

كي لا أستنشق أجسادكم الميتة حولي..

أوقفي مرافقة الملائكة لي

كي لا تسرق أوراق عمري كما حدث مع قصائدي

ولأشتم كثيراً دون هزّة من جناحها.

لا تغسلي شفتي رجاءً

ثروتي تلك القبل التي لم أكذب فيها أبداً

ولا تُكَبّري بإلهك حين أبتسم

لست سوى هازئة من عملية التطهير هذه.

فأنا أحب خطاياي كلها

ادفنوها معي

إنها سلوتي الوحيدة حين أُبعث غريبة

كما كنت دائماً هنا.

أحب رُكبتيّ العَصِيّتين على التعديل

اتركوها هكذا

لا تَضفروا شعري الطويل، أحبهُ هكذا أشعث، غاضباً

لا أريد توديع البيت

الذي متُّ فيه عشرات المرات

لن أشتاق لأي ركن فيه

وفِّروا جهودكم

دعوا يومي الأخير بينكم يمر بسلام

ورددوا اسمي فأنا لم أعد جنازةً بعد الآن

أرجوكم لا أحب البياض المشاع

ليكن كفني أحمرَ

لدي رزمة مناسبة من الخطوط الحمر التي تجاوزتها

ضمّوها جميعها إلى صدري هم أطفالي الذين خلفوني كل يوم

ومددوني على جنبي الأيسر، أخيراً وأبداً و قريباً جداً من قلبي

---

[2]القصيدة محاكاة لثقافة الدفن عند المسلمين

No Excuse Needed

To sleep whenever you want
For slumber to take you seamlessly away
from the webs of dead spiders in your head
And whenever you finish your gentle dreams,
to wake upon a window flirting with a beam of light
that dries out the nighttime nakedness of a garden

To close your door whenever you want,
and to open it if you seek a different breath
To walk on your own two feet
without looking around
For your tear to freeze like the frost of Michigan
before it exhausts your eyeballs

To smile simply
To not feel guilt when you chuckle
To stand without anxiety while your passport is stamped
To know the itinerary of your trip
and not fear talking about your life
with the stranger traveling by your side
To talk about your sorrows,
as if singing a folkloric note,
then thank the audience gleefully and proceed

To eat your bread flavored with friends' non-betrayal
on a long and winding road
To look in the mirror daily
and remark: Thank you for everything

Where then does pain find the audacity
to sit in my living room with that face?
In one sentence:
Pain needs no excuse

ليس على الألم حرج

أن تنام متى ما تشاء
وأن يأخذك السهاد سريعاً
من شبكة عناكب موتٍ في رأسك.
وتستيقظ متى ما انتهيت من أحلامك اللطيفة
على نافذة تغازل شعاعاً
يجفف عري حديقة في ليلتها.
أن تقفل بابك متى ما أردت
وتفتحه كلما أردت تنفساً مغايراً،
أن تمشي على قدميك
دون أن تلتفت،
أن تتجمد الدمعة كما صقيع مشيغان
قبل أن تورق من مقلتيك،
أن تبتسم ببساطة
وألّا تشعر بذنب حين تقهقه،
أن تقف بلا قلق أمام ختم جوازك
أن تعرف مسرى رحلتك
وألّا تخاف من الحديث عن حياتك
مع مسافر غريب بجانبك.
أن تتحدث عن أحزانك
كأنك تطرب مقاماً من الفولكلور
ثم تشكر المستمعين ببهجة وتمضي.
أن تتناول خبزك بنكهة أصدقاء لم يخونوك
في درب طويل ومتعرج.
أن تنظر في المرآة كل يوم
وتعلّق "شكراً على كل شيء"
فمن أين للألم هذا الوجه
ليجلس في صالة بيتي
بعبارة واحدة:
"ليس على الألم حرج"

Poems by Becky Thompson

Translated by Mootacem B. Mhiri

Translator's Reflection

Translating the poetry of Becky Thompson from English into Arabic may seem counter-intuitive considering that both of us are US academics and our primary audience is Anglophone. Yet, long before she compiled her 2022 collection, *To Speak in Salt*, Thompson's enthusiasm to conduct poetry workshops with refugees, who did not speak much English, was so inspiring to me. Thompson was keen to make world poetry available to people in transit (in China, Thailand, and Greece) and encourage people to write and read in their own languages during the workshops. Her generosity inspires my desire to extend a similar hand to people forced to leave their homelands, in hopes of building bridges and expressing human solidarity with them. My translation of Thompson's poetry into Arabic, the language that a large segment of the dispossessed of today's world claims as their native tongue, is hence an extension of the same sense of community and solidarity that inspires Thompson's work — that is, her activism with and on behalf of the refugees *along with* her poetry. In the end, we want Thompson's poems to reach both Arab refugees and broader Arab audiences, whose stories, struggles, and hope Thompson's poetry captures so lovingly, ever so gently, and deeply.

"Ahmad Talks to His 13-Year-Old Brother," with its original cape-shape form and its series of direct commends, exhorts Ahmad to hold his head high, to take pride in his cultural heritage, and never to give up hope. In terms of poetic style, the commands lend themselves well to translation into Arabic because the Arabic tradition is replete with exhortation poetry. I could cite multiple examples, both from pre-Islamic and from neoclassical poetry, of poems exhorting a knight or a tribesman to accomplish expected feats of courage and nobility, to come to the rescue of a damsel in distress, or to honor the codes of hospitality and goodwill. Similarly, in the poetry of such modern bards as Ahmad Shawqi, one encounters such well-known lines as the one in which the poet urges his audiences to honor teachers as the successors of prophets for what they do to refine the minds and moral character of generations of knowledge seekers. I found inspiration in those poetic models, and I tried to capture this Arabic poetic idiom in my translation of Thompson's poetry. I may have even taken some poetic license—with Thompson's permission—when translating the following lines: "Learn / how to be a barber. Wherever you go / men will need their hair cut." My Arabic translation adds a new meaning that may have not been originally there, but one that Arabic readers will readily recognize and appreciate because it evokes the same cultural pride that Thompson evoked in the preceding line. My Arabic translation of those lines goes as follows: "Learn the trade of the barber. Wherever you land / men's towering heads will bend down to you."[1] They literally bend their heads for a haircut and metaphorically bow in respect and admiration, acknowledging the nobility of Ahmad's cultural pedigree.

By contrast, translating a narrative poem like "We Leave Magnolias in a Fountain" is not an easy undertaking. My goal was to preserve the economy, directness, and simplicity of the English-language original without resorting to literal translation and without scarifying the subtle lyricism of Thompson's poetic voice. It is my hope that I managed to remain faithful to the original English poems and also appeal to Arab readers, who will encounter a unique contemporary American poetic voice that feels their pain and stands in solidarity with their unwarranted predicament and especially their courage.

---

[1] Editor's note: The line breaks in the Arabic translation differ from those in the English original.

Ahmed Talks to His 13-Year-Old Brother

Remember you are Superman, with a hurt-proof cape. Don't forget your aunt
nicknamed you balloon—he who will float above danger. Learn to draw a map
of Syria in ink on paper cups. Don't look at the sea if it makes you sad. Look
at the sea and remember you made it. Be the song you sang on the raft.
Don't run from ghosts. Use your backpack as a pillow, a seat, a table.
Carry your prayer rug inside. It's okay to let the rug double as a bed.
Eat meals with the young Palestinians. They've been through this
longer than you have. Keep ironing your shirts even though you
gotta stand in line. Know your people are proud. Remember
why they sent you first. Don't trade your toothpaste for
cigarettes. Well maybe sometimes. Don't sell your
kidney to anyone. Ever. Remember your uncle
before the sniper. Be tall. Know you come
from a people of maps and stars. Learn
how to be a barber. Wherever you go
men will need their hair cut.
Don't drink bleach.
Don't drink bleach.

تذكّر أنك سوبرمان وأنّك تملك عباءته الخارقة. لا تنسى أن عمتك أطلقت عليك لقب البالون الذي يسمو مرتفعا فوق كل الأخطار. تعلّم كيف ترسم خريطة سوريا بالحبر على الكؤوس الورقية.

ولا تنظر باتجاه البحر إذا كان ذلك ينشر الحزن في نفسك. بل أنظر إليه متذكرا أنّك نجوتَ من أذاه. كن مثل الأنشودة التي أنشدتها وأنت على الزورق. ولا تفزع من أشباح الماضي. اِتخذ من حقيبتك وسادة ومقعدا وطاولة، واحمل داخلها سجادة الصلاة.

ولا بأس إن افترشت تلك السجادة للنوم أيضا. تقاسم الرغيف مع أولئك الشبّان الفلسطينيين، فهم قد خبروا هذا المصير أطول منك. ولا تتوقف عن كيّ قمصانك حتى وإن كنت ستقف بها في صف توزيع الطعام. كن واثقا أنك سليل شعبٍ أبيّ وتذكر لماذا دفع بك أهلك للهروب قبلهم. لا تقايض معجون أسنانك ببعض السجائر وإن فعلت، فلا تدأب على ذلك. ولا تبعْ كليتك لأي أحد أبدا وتذكر استبسال عمك في مواجهة القنّاص. وارفع رأسك

وأعلم أنك من أمة قد خبرت علوم الخرائط والنجوم.

ثمّ تعلم صنعة الحلاقة، فإنك حيثما حللتَ

اِنحنت لك هامات الرجال.

لا تتجرّع سائل تبييض الملابس.

لا تفعل ذلك!

We Leave Magnolias in a Fountain

i. I write to Huda

who I met on the shore four years ago on a crowded
July day, and ask her advice for people now waiting
in Kara Tepe, since I live in a US houseboat, floating in

> some reality far from a container stuck on a hillside in
>   Mytilini,
> too hot for summer, too cold for winter, designed to entice
> madness, at the least, a yearning, sometimes hatred for what
> people
> can / not do for each other.

The two haiku she sends:

> Advice for people
> in the camps is a question
> I carry now.
>
> How could I hate Greece
> so much now, after loving
> her in Syria?

A UNHCR report: the average person needs 2,000 calories
per day to survive. So officials distribute 1,900.

Just enough less to keep you on edge?

Who do you borrow calories from? The baby? The elder?
The full-breasted woman?

ii. I write Bashir

ask him what he remembers from the sea. He writes back, no
    matter who you are, what country
you came from, if smugglers kept you in a truck for weeks, if you
    dodged fire in Kabul, if you
carried your elder aunt . . . no matter what, the sea was the worst,
    our arrival, the gift:

disaster the sea / glorious, the shore

the chop . . . the pitch . . . the storm / the hands . . . the rope . . .
    the sand
my daughter curls inside my vest / she runs with pipits by the rocks

gasoline soaks our tired clothes / wildflowers preach to a quiet
    beach

sarin gas on frightened skin / we leave magnolias in a fountain.

iii. I write a supervisor

about translator rates so we can teach Darwish and Jordan in the
    poetry class.
It is customary, he says, to pay five euro per hour. The teachers only
    get ten.
If you pay more, you send a confusing message.

The translator arrives, a professor in Afghanistan, his perfectly
    clipped
beard, his British English, he who speaks and writes in Pashto,
Urdu, Persian, and Hindi.

When my eyes say help, after people start to fidget, after the whiteboard
marker gives up, after we run out of pencils, he begins to recite Nye
in Dari so those who can't read might float a poem above their chairs.

iv. after class, my energy evaporated, I ask, where will you rest?

Back at my container, safer than the forest
where we cowered when they fired on us
and better than forty-five days in an Iranian jail.

He shows a photo of his wife, her gardenia petal nails
scrubbing his oxford-button shirt.

Their container is white tin on the outside, white tin
on the inside, no insulation. No electricity. No internet.
No rugs. No windows. No sky.

We're lucky. We are here.

v. the view from Mytilini

a holiday for the wealthy.
I take the bus back to Eftalou.
Gaze out a window
scratched by granite and salt.

أزهار الماغنوليا في نافورة

1. أكتب رسالة إلى هدى

التي اِلتقيتها أول مرة منذ أربع سنوات
عند الشاطئ في يوم تموزي مشهود.
أسألها النصيحة لمن لا يزالون عالقين في "كراتبي"
فأنا أعيش في منزل عائم في الولايات المتحدة
وأسبح في عوالم أبعد ما تكون عن واقع

حاوية عالقة على أحد جوانب هضبة في "متليني".
حاوية مثل الفرن صيفا و مثل صناديق الثلج في الشتاء
صناديق مصممة لتدفعك بسرعة نحو الجنون،
أو لتثير فيك على الأقل حنينا وأحيانا أخرى نفورا ممّا يفعله
أو ما لا يفعله الإنسان من أجل أخيه الإنسان.

كان ردّها الآتي:

اِسداء النصح للعالقين في المخيم بات حملا يقل كاهلي.
كيف يمكنني أن أكنّ كلّ هذا الكره لليونان ،
بعد كل المحبّة التي كنت أكنّها له عندما كنت في سوريا؟

تقرير منظمة الأمم المتحدة للاجئين:
يحتاج الإنسان إلى معدل ألفي حريرة في اليوم ليبقى على قيد الحياة.
لذلك لا يوزع المسئولون سوى ألف و تسعمئة حريرة في اليوم،

وهو مقدار كاف لتظل متأرجحا على حافة سوء التغذية.

ومن أين ستحصل على باقي احتياجاتك؟
أ تحصل عليها من الرضيع أم من المسن أم من المرأة المرضعة؟

2. أكتب إلى بشير

أسأله عمّا ظلّ عالقا بذاكرته من تجربة البحر.

فيردّ بشير: ليس مهما مَن تكون ولا مِن أي بلد أتيت

ليس مهما إن كان المهرّبون قد تركوك عالقا في شاحنة لأسابيع،

أو كيف كنت تتفادى رصاص القناصة في كابول

حاملا قريبتك المسنة على ظهرك . . . مهما كانت الملابس

كلّها أهوَن من ركوب البحر وأهواله

أمّا الوصول الى اليابسة فهوغاية المنى.

البحر فاجعة / الشاطئ نجاة

تلاطُم الأمواج العاتية . . . العاصفةُ / الأيادي . . . الحبال . . . الرمال

تتكوّر صغيرتي داخل سترة النجاة بدلا من أن تطارد الطيور الصغيرة عند الصخور

ويبلّل البنزين ثيابنا المهترئة في حين تناجي الأزهار البرّية سكون الشواطئ.

وينشر غاز السارين الرعب في مسامّنا بينما ننشر نحن أزهار الماغنوليا في احدى النافورات.

3. أكتب إلى أحد المسؤولين

أساله عن تكلفة الاستعانة بمترجم، حتّى يتسنّى لنا أن ندرس شعر درويش وجوردن في ورشة الشعر.

تعودنا على دفع خمس دولارات في الساعة كان جوابه.

الأساتذة فقط يحصلون على عشرة.

قد تُثيرين البلبلة إن أنتِ دفعتِ أكثر من ذلك.

ويأتي المترجم، أستاذ سابق من أفغانستان

بِلحيته الأنيقة وبِلَكْنَتِه البريطانيّة

ومهارة في التكلّم والكتابة بالباشتو والأُرديّة والفارسيّة والهنديّة.

وعندما تسأله نظراتي متوسّلةً العون،

حينما يبدأ الحاضرون في التململ ويتوقّف قلم السبورة البيضاء عن الكتابة وتنكسر كل الاقلام،

عندها فقط ينطلق المترجم في إلقاء قصائد ناي[2]

باللغة الدّاريّة لِيتمكّن من لا يستطيع القراءة من الحاضرين أن يتمسّك ولو بخيط من خيوط الشّعر

فيحلّق مرتفعا فوق الكراسي.

---

[2] إشارة الى الشاعرة الأمريكيّة من أصل فلسطيني نعومي شهاب ناي

4. بعد إنتِهاء الورشة، أسأله وقد خارت كلَّ قِوايَ: أين سَتستريحُ؟

"في حاويَتي، فهي أضمن من الغابة التي كُنّا نتوارى فيها
عندما كانوا يطلقون علينا النار،
وهي أفضل من خمسة وأربعين يوما قضيناها في سجن ايرانيّ."

بعد ذلك يُريني صورةً لزوجته التي طلت أظافرُها بلون زهرة الغاردينيا،
وهي منهمكة في فرك قميصه ذي الأكمام الطويلة بين يديها.

الحاوية صندوق من الصفيح الأبيض من الداخل ومن الخارج
ليس فيها عازل حراري ولا كهرباء ولا انترنت.
ليس فيها سجّاد وليس فيها نوافذ. بلا أفق.

نحن محظوظون مادُمْنا على قيد الحياة.

5. المَشهد من "متليني"

يوم راحة للأثرياء.
أركب الحافلة عائدة الى "اِفتالو"
وألقي نظرة من النافذة
التي أحدثت الصخور البركانيّة والملح خدوشا في بلّورها.

Poems by Saadi Youssef

Translated by Khaled Mattawa

Translator's Reflection

I dove into Saadi Youssef's work in the early nineties. Before then, his name had rung a bell that I did not know what to associate with. When I began to read Youssef's work attentively, my impression was that it was akin to a revelation, the sort of poetry that I was waiting for, a quieter, more engaging poetry whose only argument is the poet's experience of life. This is what I saw, this is how things smelled and felt and tasted. It was a disarming sort of poetry that I had not encountered in Arabic or anywhere else when I was just becoming interested in poetry. At that time, translation was the great siren beckoning and luring me toward Arabic poetry and, in the process, making me "practice" poetry more, in the same way that a violinist practices their instrument by playing the music of better and better composers.

Translating Youssef's work made us friends. He was hesitant at first but believed in the work because I was committed to it. I used to mail him snail-mail letters, to a PO Box in Jordan, to which he promptly replied. I used to also call a number in Amman when he seemed to disappear. It turned out to be a number at the Ministry of Tourism. I never figured out the connection. And despite becoming great friends once he settled in London, I never found out.

Youssef was easy to work with because, for one thing, he knew English well. But more importantly, he was also a translator, and he appreciated the effort of translation. He made very few comments on my translations and allowed me to choose what I liked from among his poems. I felt free and supported by a great poet. The poems in this selection are from Youssef's last decade of writing. I wanted to return to him to honor his work but also to share with the English-reading world the work of a true and diligent master of poetry.

Will We Learn?

What do you see from the window of a plane flying,
soaring higher than a star?

You know the clouds, you live among them.
And what appears as a reflection of the sea,
you understand as physics.
As for the games the trees play,
it's hard to tell from these heights.
Elevation has done its heinous act again.
If only you'd never soared,
never flown,
never had a pair of wings.

The clouds are beautiful
and the sea
and trees.
Understand, my son.
Get it into your head.
Don't wade far into blindness!

هل نتعلّمُ؟

ماذا ترى من كوّةٍ في جسمٍ طائرةٍ تُحَـــلّقُ عالياً، أعلى من النجمِ؟

الغيومُ تكادُ تعرفُها لأنك ساكنٌ فيها
وما يبدو من البحرِ انعكاساً، أنتَ تفهمُهُ من الفيزياءِ
أمّا لُعبةُ الأشجارِ فهي من الأعالي غيرُ واضحةٍ . . .
لقد فعَلَ الـعُلــوُّ الفِعلةَ الشنعاءَ
ليتكَ لم تُحَـلّقْ
لم تَطِرْ
لم تمتلك يوماً جناحَينِ . . .

الغيومُ جميلةٌ
والبحرُ
والأشجارُ .
فافهَمْ يا بُنَيّ . . .
افهَمْ
ولا تذهبْ بعيداً في العمـاءِ!

Blissful Sleep

If I miss a country, I can fly to it
or even try to swim there.
But, to be honest, I am tired of longing
and remembrance.
Nostalgia is no longer my song.
The countries have become alike.
I know what I'll see here and there
as if I were traveling the lines of my palm,
as if I'm always on the same old bald plateau.
Year after year, I have walked streets I had walked before,
even as I realize that I had not been there before.
I look out now:
This street takes to the sea,
this street ends at a river,
and this street leads me to desolation?
What now?
I will pull the sheet over my head and, contented, will close my
    eyes.
Then I will wander, all alone, to sleep.

نومُ الهناءةِ

لو كنتُ مشتاقاً إلى بلدٍ لَطِـــــرْتُ إليهِ

أو حاولتُ أن أمضي إليه سِـــباحةً . . .

لكنني ، وأقولُها صِدْقاً ، سَئِمْتُ الشوقَ

والذكرى

ولم يَعُد الحنينُ لديّ أغنيةً .

تشابهَت البلادُ

وصرتُ أعرفُ ما سألقى ههنا أو ههنا

حتى كأني راحلٌ في راحَتَـيّ . . .

كأنني في الهضْبةِ الصلعاءِ إيّاها .

وعاماً بعدَ آخرَ ، صرتُ أمشي في شوارعَ قد مشَيتُ بها

وإنْ أدركتُ أني لم أكُنْ فيها ولو يوماً . . .

أُطِلُّ الآنَ:

هذا شارعٌ يمضي إلى بحرٍ

وهذا شارعٌ يُفضي إلى نهرٍ . . .

وهذا شارعٌ قد كان طوَّحَ بي إلى قفْرٍ

وماذا ؟

سوف ، أسحبُ ، هانئاً ، طرَفَ الـمُـلاءةِ

أغمِضُ العينينِ

ثمّ أهيمُ ، وحدي ، كي أنامْ . . .

Word Games

Perhaps the sky you'd hoped for has abandoned you . . .
Perhaps!
Let's get the suitcase ready:
There's a heavenly sky (You've exhausted her talking about it so
    much!)
And then there's a sky for people.
Tell me,
to which one are you returning?
Where do you feel most comfortable?
To which do you hand over your head, surrendering it, like a
    pillow?
No!
Don't say: "Is this an interrogation now?"
I am your friend,
your image,
a copy of you.
Now, none of us will deceive the other.
Now we are equal
like the teeth of that famous man's comb.
We are equals
You haven't forgotten that I am a communist
(And you didn't forget that you were a communist too)
So let's agree!
Let's say, at least,
that transcendence has nothing to do with the sky.

ألعابٌ لُغَـويّـةٌ

رّبما هجرتْكَ السماءُ التي كنتَ ترجو . . .

رّبما !

فلْتَعُدْ للحقيبة :

ثَمّ سـماءٌ سماويّةٌ (أنتَ أرهقتَها بالحديث طويلاً !)

وثَمّ السماءُ التي هي للناسِ .

قُل لي :

إلى أيّ واحدةٍ أنتَ ترجِعُ

أو تستريحُ ؟

إلى أيّ واحدةٍ أنتَ تُسْـلِمُ رأسَكَ ، مستسلِماً ، كالوسادةِ ؟

لا !

لا تَقُل لي : أمُسْتَنطِقي أنتَ ؟

إني صديقُكَ

صورتُكَ

النسخةُ . . .

الآنَ ، لن يخدعَ الواحدُ ، الآخرَ .

الآنَ نحنُ سواسيةٌ

مثلَ أسنانِ مشطِكَ ذاكَ الـمُثَلَّـمِ . . .

نحن سواسيةٌ

أنت لم تنسَ أني الشيوعيُّ

(لم تنسَ أنكَ كنتَ الشيوعيَّ)

فلنتّفِقْ !

لِنَقُلْ ، في الأقلّ ، بأنّ التّساميَ ليس السماء . . .

Training Plane Crosses the Window

The training plane returning to the flight school
flew past my window, waning, like a bird.
The sky is white
and trees bare.
And I, the poor one, shivering in my room
almost saw snow falling around me—
white meteors falling,
pages from books falling,
dresses of women I loved falling,
milk teeth falling,
the history of a country falling.
....
....
....
What did the training plane do?
The freshman pilot
will enter another school
and soon he'll
happily
toss away his bombs
and kill the poor souls tending Basra's date palms.

طائرةُ تدريبٍ تعبرُ النافذة

طائرةُ التدريبِ العائدةُ الآنَ إلى مدرسةِ الطيَّرانِ
تَعَدَّتْ نافذتي ، متضائلةً ، كالطيرِ . . .
سماءٌ بيضاءُ
وأشجارٌ عاريةٌ
وأنا ، المسكينَ ، أُقَفْقِفُ في الغرفة
حتى كدتُ أرى ثلجاً يَسّاقَطُ حولي ؛
شُهُباً بيضاً تَسّاقَطُ
أوراقاً من كُتُبٍ تَسّاقَطُ
أثوابَ نساءٍ كنتُ عشقْتُ ، قديماً ، تَسّاقَطُ
أسناناً لَبَناً تَسّاقَطُ
تاريخَ بلادٍ يَسّاقَطُ . . .

. . . .

. . . .

. . . .

ماذا فعلتْ طائرةُ التدريبِ العابرةُ ؟
الطيَّارُ الـغِرُّ
سيدخلُ مدرسةً أخرى
وسيقذفُ كلَّ قنابلِهِ
وهو سعيدٌ . . .
يَقتلُ فلاَّحي نخلِ البصرة !

Iraq Is Coming

A beautiful Iraq will come.
Iraq will come
after the American leaves
and the attendant Persian servant is gone.
This beautiful Iraq
is coming in the air we breathe,
in tea at the heights of the Euphrates,
in the bitter arak at the riverfront.
This beautiful Iraq
is coming in the cape of my mother, who passed away, while I knew
    nothing of her
passing
(I was footing it through the alleys of Paris).
This wondrous Iraq
will bring us home from our hovels in countries we did not love
and whose people do not like our features
or the ferocity of our bodies.
We will be happy,
trembling,
barefoot,
light,
full of chastity
and horror.
We will say:
O Iraq, O nation,
the world has no room
for our endless separation.
O Iraq . . .

العراقُ آتٍ

سوف يأتي العراقُ الجميل
سوف يأتي العراق
بعدَ أن يرحلَ الأمريكيُّ
والخادمُ الفارسيُّ الـمُعَـمَّـمُ . . .
هذا العراقُ الجميل
قادمٌ في الهواءِ الذي نتنفّسُ
في الشاي عند أعالي الفرات
وفي العَرَقِ الـمُرِّ في جبهةِ النهرِ . . .
هذا العراق الجميل
قادمٌ في عباءةِ أُمّي التي رحلتْ وأنا جاهلٌ أنها رحلتْ
(كنتُ أذرعُ زنْقاتِ باريسَ) . . .
هذا العراقُ العجيب
سوف يأتي بنا من مَنـابِذنا في الديارِ التي لم نُحِبّ
الديارِ التي لم تُحِبّ ملامحَنا
وضراوةَ أجسادِنا . . .
ولَسوفَ نكونُ سعيدينَ
مرتجفينَ
حُفاةً
خِفافاً
وممتلئينَ عفافاً
ورُعباً . . .
وسوف نقولُ لهُ :
أيُّهذا العراق
لم يَعُدْ في الطبيعةِ مُتَّسَـعٌ
للفراقْ
أيُّهذا العراقْ . . .

Poems by Sara Abou Rashed

Translated by Sara Abou Rashed

Translator's Reflection

To translate is to crack open a language, or two; to self-translate is to do so while shattered in the first place. On a recent drive from Dearborn, Michigan, to my American home of Columbus, Ohio, it occurred to me that foreignness is the ability to compare. I found myself incapable of looking at the vastness of this country, its highways and city skylines and cornfields, without recalling my past lives—in Damascus, Syria, and the inherited past life of my grandparents in Haifa, Palestine—and wrestling against their multiplicity. Here there are too many churches even for a small town. There, the countryside feels more hidden from public view. Here, there. Here, there. Here. There. Here. There. Language is a similar ordeal. I cannot imagine what it feels like to know only one, to express my thoughts in only one register, octave, rhythm, alphabet. Perhaps we—multilinguals—come to cultivate consciousnesses greater than the singularity of each of our languages. I memorize scientific terms in English by tying them to similar-sounding words in Arabic, or reflect on the roots of a Syrian idiom and find its exact resonance in French. In my mind, the shattering makes for irreplicable mosaics, small pockets of wonder and light. Incoherent sentences. Incomprehensible puns. Certainly, occupation and my move across the world were only a further shattering, out of which the following poems emerged. These poems attempt to translate—transgress—the bounds of one another by rewriting themselves into a peculiar space, the cracking between worlds.

In Arabic, The Word for "Hope" Is Similar to "Pain"

There was a time when
the dead were counted
by full body, and violence
came with a warning sign.

Now, joy is a foreigner
on TV screens. To a head-
line's left, a smart scale capable
of rough estimates.

في اللغة العربية، كلمة "أمل" تشبه "ألم"

كان هناك زمن
يُعد فيه الموتى
بأجسادٍ تامة والعنف يأتي
مع لافتة إنذار.
الآن، البهجة غريبة
عن شاشات التلفاز.
يسار كل رأسـ
ية خبر صحفي، عداد ذكي
يجيد التقدير التقريبي.

Let Me Put It Another Way

War to me

is dementia to my memories;
I'm writing to forget.

Exile is an elderly woman weeping
because she has forgotten her name;
I'm writing to remind her.

دعني أشرحها بطريقة أخرى

الحرب بالنسبة لي
كاضطراب فقدان الذاكرة بالنسبة لذكرياتي:
أكتب كي أنسى.

أمّا المنفى فامرأة عجوز تبكي
لأنها نسيت اسمها:
أكتب لأذكّرها.

Lineage

In 1910, I am told, a woman in my family
didn't recognize her own husband after
seven years of war. When he first saw her
outside her door with a daughter half her height,
he asked, "Lady, do you know someone who
lived here, was left with a newborn,
and went by this name?"

✦ ✦ ✦

"I am her," I want my daughter to say
when the apartheid wall falls. "I am her,
or what remains of the story."
Over seven decades away, searching,
surely, someone or something awaits.
A rusty keyhole, an olive-skinned doll,
a stool in the middle of the road.

نسب

قيل لي، في عام 1910، أن امرأة من عائلتي
لم تميّز زوجها بعد سبع سنوات
من الحرب. حين رآها للمرة الأولى
على باب دارها مع ابنة تصل لنصف طولها،
سألها، "سيدتي، أتعرفين امرأة كانت تسكن هنا
تُركت مع رضيعة وتسمى.. . . . ؟"

✦ ✦ ✦

"أنا هي" أود أن تجيب ابنتي
حين ينهال جدار الفصل العنصري.
"أنا هي أو ما تبقى من القصة!"
أكثر من سبعة عقود مضت، مبعدون، باحثون،
حتماً لا زال شخصٌ أو شيءٌ ينتظر:
ثقب مفتاح صدئ، دمية حنطية البشرة
كرسي في منتصف الطريق.

I'm Told I Have a Clear Sense of Purpose

There is no room in my house
for uselessness. I have lost.
Years ago, in ceramics class,

my friends shaped mud
into asymmetrical statues,
called them pure art, abstract decor.

I made dishes, a toothbrush holder,
a jewelry box and its lid.
Don't blame me, even the screws

in my walls carry more weight
than intended. On the internet,
I found videos of my house

turned museum for what isn't there.
My old kitchen now a skeleton,
bones stripped naked

of cement and copper wires. Still,
I don't curse the revolution, the war,
the thieves or the regime; I curse only

myself—all these cracked tiles
and the probable risk of death
by electrocution for a day's
worth of bread.

يقال أن لدي حس عالٍ بنفعية الأشياء

ليس هنالك مكان في منزلي
لعدم الجدوى. سبق وأن خسرت.
منذ سنين، في صف السيراميك،

حوّل أصدقائي الطين إلى تماثيل
غير متناظرة. نعتوهم بالفن الرفيع،
الديكور المجرد.

أما أنا فصنعت أطباقاً وحاملة لفرش الأسنان.
صنعت صندوق مجوهرات وغطاءً له.
لا تلمني، فحتى المسامير

في جدراني تحمل أكثر من الوزن
المخصص. على الانترنت،
وجدت فيديوهات لمنزلي

وقد تحول إلى متحف لكل ما هو غائب.
مطبخي القديم بات هيكلاً،
كومة عظامٍ عارية

من الاسمنت والأسلاك النحاسية. مع هذا،
لا ألعن الثورة، ولا الحرب، ولا اللصوص
ولا حتى النظام. ألعن فقط

نفسي—كل هذا البلاط المُكسّر
واحتمالية خطر الموت صعقاً
بالكهرباء جلب كمية خبز كافية
ليوم واحد لا غير.

Rachid Niny[1]

From *Journal of a Clandestine Migrant*

Translated by Angela Haddad

---

[1] Editor's note: "Niny" is the author's preferred transliteration of his name. However, it is often also written as "Nini," as in the two Works Cited entries below.

Translator's Reflection

Rachid Niny's *Yawmiyyāt Muhājir Sirrī* (Journal of a clandestine migrant), published in 1999, recounts the precarity and difficulties of undocumented migrants in Spain. Throughout, it evokes the experience of *harrāga*, a Maghrebi term derived from the verb "to burn" which is used to label migrants who cross the Mediterranean Sea—often under hazardous conditions—and burn their documents upon arrival to make immediate deportation to their countries of origin more difficult if they are discovered by authorities. Indeed, the first page of the book visually recalls the term as Niny watches a news segment on television about several migrants' fatal attempt to cross sea on a small boat, and the text repeatedly draws attention to migrants burning their documents.

The word *Yawmiyyāt*, which can be translated as "journal" or "diary," seemingly positions the work as a first-person reflection on the lives of such migrants. Niny sketches out the poor living conditions and the physically demanding labor in fields or behind establishment doors to which he and other migrants from low-income and marginalized regions are subjugated. He also illustrates the constant negotiation of relations with other marginalized communities like the Roma and poor Spaniards while also contemplating the ease with which wealthy tourists from Northern Europe vacation in Spain. While some commentators have opted to translate the title's first word as "diary," the text's non-linearity, irregularity in terms of installments, and reflective mode lend weight to the word "journal" as a translation. Rather than recounting daily events, Niny contemplates the forms of labor, types of sociality, and places available to *harrāga* as various borders and boundaries cross their ways.

The second part of the title, which can be literally translated as "of a Secret Migrant," avoids the specificity of *harrāga* as a term (whose singular would be *harrāg*). Unlike the only full translation of the book, which exists in Spanish as *Diario de un ilegal* (Diary of an illegal immigrant, 2002), I concur with David Álvarez's usage of "clandestine migrant" in his analysis of the work, as the description conveys the layered meanings contained in the word *sirrī* (secret) in the context of the book. As depicted in the excerpt below, Niny attempts to maintain a low profile to escape discovery by law enforcement authorities as an undocumented migrant. While *sirrī* can be translated as "undocumented," as opposed to derogatory adjectives like "illegal," it does not account for the second form of secrecy in the text, which is only revealed at the end. Niny's migration, he confesses, is not driven by necessity, but by the possibility of a challenge. Contrary to the experience of *ḥarrāga*, Niny enters Spain on a journalist's visa under the pretext of covering a conference on the Berber community and becomes an "undocumented" migrant only after he overstays his visa. Even when that point is reached, he never fully does away with his passport and manages to publicly report his activity in the press, albeit in Arabic. In fact, before appearing as a book, the work's contents appeared in a series of articles that Niny began writing in 1997 for *al-ʿAlam*, the daily newspaper of Morocco's Istiqlal Party, in order to provide an account of what Moroccan and other migrants arriving from the Maghreb faced on the other side of the Mediterranean. In this sense, "clandestine" operates between two points: "undocumented," on the one hand, and "covert" or "undercover," on the other.

In addition to highlighting the uncontrollable conditions that affect an undocumented migrant's daily wages, this translated excerpt is a reflection on Niny's positionality as an Arabic-speaking migrant from North Africa. This positionality is further complicated by Spain's history, which was shaped by the conquest of the Americas as well as the Spanish Crown's expulsion of Muslim and Jewish populations from what used to be Muslim-ruled Iberia during the *Reconquista*. Upon his arrival, Niny is labeled by Spaniards not as a Moroccan or migrant worker, but as a "Moro" or Moor, a term that accrued derogatory connotations in reference to Muslims during the late medieval and early modern periods. The summoning of this category of differentiation from *Reconquista* narratives points to contemporary actors' demarcations of self and other through residual ideologies or, at the very least, their terminologies. The differentiations between who can be seen as Spanish and not are put on stark display during a multiday, whitewashed festival in Benidorm that Niny attends called *Moros y Cristianos*, or "Moors and Christians." However, through language, writing, and allusions to certain figures in Arab history and Arabic literature, Niny simultaneously re-establishes his identity as a cultural and social critic and reclaims the figure of the Moor within frames relevant to his educational formation rather than the lingering idiom of the *Reconquista*, even, as will be seen below, in its most romantic iterations.

Works Cited

Álvarez, David. "Recording Daily Life in the Margins of History and of the Nation: Rachid Nini's *Diary of a Clandestine Migrant.*" *Biography* 36, no. 1 (2013): 148–178.

Nini, Rachid. *Diario de un ilegal.* Translated by Malika Embarek López and Gonzalo Fernández Parrilla. Madrid: Ediciones del Oriente y del Mediterráneo, 2002.

From *Journal of a Clandestine Migrant*

(4)

We didn't work for two days straight. We drank Manolo's awful coffee and then got to the field by seven, only to find the trees dripping wet and the sky overcast. It poured down an hour or so later. The guys were playing cards back at Merche's bar and having a good time. Merche was piggishly devouring chocolate and staring at the TV. No one had drowned today. "Things must be getting better," she jeered. I told her not to be so quick and that tomorrow she'd be proven wrong. People risk their lives every day. By land. On sea. Everywhere. I'm terrified that I'll see one of my friends' corpses floating in the water one day on TV. It'll be awful.

On the way back through the mountains yesterday, Merche said that her friend asked for a crate of oranges to bring to her dying father in Murcia, so she stopped by one of the fields and stole three crates. The whole way she kept talking about her youngest daughter, Sandra. A fortune teller told her that she had a special gift and could see things. I only ever see trees through the window, I said. Merche chuckled and said that was good. At least her daughter's future would be set. She lingered on the word "future," and I thought a bit about mine. I didn't see anything. The future is a place bereft of light, or it's a poorly lit one. That's why everything seems murky in it. At least I know what my immediate future will look like. It's held hostage by the rain, the morning fog, the sunrise, the trees, and Fernando the truck driver who comes by with empty crates and leaves with them filled with oranges at night. Well, the weather has to be clear and sunny and Fernando needs to stop drinking and leave the bar before eight for that last bit to happen.

It had been days since Cristián came to work. When Merche brought him in the morning in the car, he said that he started working again at the Italian restaurant that he had worked at before, though the restaurant wouldn't open its doors until the summer. He got himself some new, white front teeth. They looked great. He started smiling without pursing his lips together. Fernando Pessoa. I don't know why, but every time Fernando the truck driver comes by, I think of Fernando Pessoa, even though they are total opposites.

Fernando the truck driver doesn't wear prescription glasses like Pessoa and drives a truck. He doesn't even write poetry. It's pretty funny.

Since the forecast called for more rain, I headed out of Oliva and went to Benidorm. No one would be working there today. Rows of chairs had been lined up in front of the coffee shops and houses and along the alleys and pathways that the procession would pass in front of. Young girls were wearing marvelously decorated gowns. Older women had painted their faces and were sitting on seats or the sidewalks in front of the coffee shops hours before the procession began. Echoes of military music made their way from a distance. I was standing in the middle of the crowd. I'm fairly tall, but the Brits were blocking everything with their huge bodies. Older Spanish women were clutching their purses and smiling. The Brits don't care about foreigners, even when their wives are eyed up by them. Their unwavering indifference baffles me.

Every year the city's streets come to life with a story called *Moros y Cristianos*. The crux of the story is that a Crusader king approaches an Arab king with his army and, standing in front of the fort's gate, convinces the Arab king to leave by reciting poems. That's how the Arab king, accompanied by his soldiers, picks up and goes, returning to his land behind the sea. Then, the Crusader king enters the fort. Every bit is narrated in poetic meter. Knights dressed as Arabs and others dressed as Crusaders face each other in mock duels at night on the beach. A knight from one of the sides prevails every evening, but on the festival's last day, the Crusader knight reigns victorious, and the Arab knight falls onto the sandy shore. The audience claps for a long time until the Arab knight rises from his death and animates the crowd. There isn't a hint of defeat in the days leading up to the finale, but it is always reserved for the Arab knight. It's witty, this way of narrating history to foreigners. Forget about telling new generations about what really happened to the Arabs when they were driven out of al-Andalus. The Inquisition. Slaughter. Collective exile. None of that would bring in tourists. It would be too dramatic for a festival. It's better that the show goes on the way it does, commemorating the expulsion of the Arabs. The Moors. A more beautiful account of exile really couldn't be told. Even the dialogues are composed of rosy verses dripping with love and peace. The show is awesome, though—beating drums, young women stringing Eastern melodies, college students everywhere, and pretty ladies in Arabic-fashioned dresses. They pretend to be Castilian bondmaids that have been captured by Arab knights advancing with pompous arrogance and brandishing their shiny swords. I was in awe for a bit. The leader of the Moors was a corpulent knight with a real beard, but his face was painted over black. Others hoped the fake beards they had fastened on would make them look like Arab knights.

The leader brandished his split-ended sword and fervently rallied the crowd. I thought of Sayyid Ali's sword that was drawn above the blackboard on yellow paper when I was in grade school. Sayyid Ali had pierced ghouls through the head with his two-pointed scimitar. The leader was riding a black horse and wore a helmet. His steps were more like those of a surveyor than of a fighter headed to war, so he didn't look afraid. He smiled and advanced.

Being there in that spectacle suddenly felt more ridiculous than the fake duel on the beach. I was also exhausted because I was going back and forth between watching the events and being on the look-out for police uniforms in case I needed to vanish into thin air. I went back home without watching the rest of the festival, but I knew the end well. The Crusader king would come with his soldiers and share a few poems he had learned by heart. The Arab king would then look down upon him from his horse and respond in crafted verse. He'd leave the fortress honorably without one drop of blood being shed. I returned home shattered. On the way back, the image of the leader of the Moorish troops in blackface flashed before my eyes. I don't know why, but I thought he resembled Antarah, whose face had been drawn above his poem—the satirical one that mocks a stingy king—in my high school's second-year reading room. I also recalled one *hakawati*'s tale that I had heard near Bab Lakhmiss in Salé. This storyteller said Antarah hadn't died in his bed like poets do today but had been killed like any real knight. The *hakawati* was surer about the anecdote than the professors of ancient literature at the university. The man said that Antarah uttered poetry as easily as he breathed and that one day there was a misunderstanding between him and a blind man. The reason being poetry, of course. The blind man was more certain of himself than Antarah was of his tongue, so he challenged him to death. Conceited about his strength, Antarah shrugged his shoulders in the vast desert and kicked his horse which, according to the *hakawati*, was as black as its owner. He added that Antarah preferred having a black horse because it would help him hide in the middle of the desert at night, but the blind man clearly made him out. He made him out from the center of his inner darkness. It was Antarah who was blind because he hadn't seen the threat of the blind man for what it was and took him for a fool. Antarah's problem was that he was so massive that his piss could be heard from miles away. One day, after an entire lifetime's chase, the blind man heard Antarah's voice among all the knights. He finally smiled and pulled an arrow out from his quiver.

Like an experienced huntsman, he aimed in the direction of the giant's voice with close precision. He pulled on the bow and let death choose its most efficient position and then released. That's how the blind man lived and Antarah died.

No one, not even the *hakawati*, knows why Antarah didn't see the danger as he neared it. Why exactly did he insist on not seeing it? Why did he refuse to notice the blind man's threats when they were clearly written all over his face? The blind most likely see past their suffering. I've never seen a blind person fall in the street, but I've laughed at people who've stumbled and fallen with their eyes wide open. I guess Antarah didn't perceive his death because he couldn't see anything aside from Abla, that woman he loved to death. He had scattered his sights in hopes of seeing her. Now we know why he preferred having a black horse. It wasn't just about not being seen. He didn't care to see anyone, let alone his death. Love is like an arrow pointed aimlessly. It's like a blind man guided by a young lady on a lit path.

I still don't know what I'd say to the police if they were to stop me in the street. Early comers would tell you not to carry your passport outside the house, unless you want someone to know your nationality. Abdelwahab says they stop him more than once a day and do a full search. Sometimes they seize his goods. I told him that if I were an officer, I'd do the same because he looks suspicious. But he said that the elderly take to him. They pity him. Or something like that. He told me that things are better in Spain now than before. Just three years ago, they'd burst into hotel rooms and send anyone they'd catch to Tangier. I told him I knew my rights well. Even though I'm here illegally, I'm not a criminal. I'm a problem asking to be solved. That's all. I told Abdelwahab this for the sake of philosophizing. Actually, I could very well be a criminal. Or at least become one.

Nisma Alaklouk

Her, Him, and Gaza

Translated by Julia Schwartz

Translator's Reflection

Gaza is a cause of nostalgia, a source of trauma, and a place to which the narrators have no plans to return in Nisma Alaklouk's "Hiyya, huwwa, wa-Ghazzah" (Her, him, and Gaza). The story's two narrators reveal disparate relationships with their shared birthplace over the course of the narrative, as they intersperse reflections on their past relationship with each other with vignettes of life in their respective adopted cities of Brussels and Antwerp. For both the unnamed male narrator and Baysan, the female narrator named after her grandfather's village in Palestine, the past and present take turns occupying the foreground of their imaginations. Baysan describes her balcony in Gaza in vivid detail: the green tea she would drink there, the way the air felt in the summer, and the precise amount of light in the streets. Memories of Gaza are inextricable from Baysan's life in Brussels in the form of both nostalgia and trauma. The lackluster view from her house in Brussels pales in comparison to the comfort and pleasure of her old balcony; fireworks on New Year's Eve induce vestiges of the terror brought on by explosions in Gaza. For the male narrator, Gaza interposes itself on a tram ride in the form of a sleeping child who strikes him as unmistakably Gazan; his reaction to this boy is the entry point to describing his longing for the scent of Gaza's air and soil.

The male narrator's second vignette also takes place in transit, on the Brussels metro, where he unexpectedly finds Baysan. The setting of his narrative on public transportation contrasts with Baysan's narration of her portion of the story from her house in Brussels. While Baysan has just moved from a studio apartment to a larger apartment and is contemplating what sort of couch to buy, the male narrator describes his house in Antwerp primarily as the site of his intrusive memories of Baysan, the place where he imagines her looking out at him from his mirror, closet, and box of books. His use of a box for book storage evokes a living space in flux, one whose inhabitant has not entirely settled in. Baysan, meanwhile, cites her expanding library as a reason for needing more space; she is determined to cultivate a home in Brussels that accommodates her belongings and needs.

Baysan is equally resolute in her efforts to extricate herself emotionally from the male narrator. She describes herself as standing halfway along a tightrope in this process, paused in a linear trajectory. The male narrator, in contrast, meanders. His narrative begins on a tram ride with no set destination, and the end point of the metro trip in his second vignette is determined by the past's imprint on him: he is traveling to an event for an author whose work Baysan introduced him to.

The male narrator's motion is stalled in the final image of the story, when the crush of passengers boarding a metro car prevents him from getting on before the doors close in his face. He is separated from Baysan, who is on the train, by a partition that is thin but nonnegotiable. For this separation he blames "the jealous metro," a machine whose scheduled route does not yield to his nostalgia. His nemesis is the brutal imposition of spatial and temporal distance.

Her, Him, and Gaza

Half a Woman

How often I savored a hot cup of tea with fresh green mint, spread out in front of the TV or on the balcony of my room on the floor there in Gaza. How often I would fling a handful of sorrows off that balcony. The sorrows would fall on their head sometimes; other times they would stick out their tongue, gloating: "You're not as clever as the others who have tried to kill me—it won't be easy for you."

These sorrows have a real mouth on them.

Here in Brussels, the houses all look alike on the outside and are all about the same height, usually no more than three stories.

I have been half a woman lately, standing halfway along a tightrope. I can't move forward in my new life or go back to him. He is waiting behind the curtain, dressed in pride and refusal. However much he exasperated me, I still did what would make him happy without even thinking about it.

When I managed, once, to crack open the sorrows' head, I stood in my place, pleased with my victory. I didn't want to go to sleep, afraid my taunting sorrows would wake up from my attempts to kill them.

How hard I tried to forget you, and couldn't. I tried to extricate myself from you many times, when I had gotten tired of longing. I started to realize then that the colors have gray and purple in their arsenal—they are not limited to black and white.

I am still myself. I love romantic TV shows. I long for my warm bed in the winter and in the summer. I am still stubborn and maybe "abrasive" by some people's standards. But I love my newfound discretion.

My old habits are decked out in deceptive new clothing. They are still lurking somewhere inside of me, waiting for their chance to come out in public.

Life is not calculations with a ruler and pen. Life would be you wearing me underneath a cloak of happiness and me fitting there comfortably, without irritations.

Nostalgia extends his hand straight toward my heart so that I breathe in his scent. I am coated in a stinging longing, on which a bath has no effect. I sense him around me everywhere; I pick up his scent and feel his touch on me all over again. I see him saunter ahead of me, then lose everything that pointed me toward him in an instant. This longing that revels in my arteries—I don't know anything like it. I have forgotten, with it, how to write a beautiful text.

My desires contradict each other. My life has become easy and difficult and has started to blend together.

Life is the way it is; it doesn't pay attention to who keeps up with it and who stands still, waiting.

This time, I won't go back. I have grown and my feelings have matured, and they are no longer satisfied with a handsome boy who struts and swaggers, or a handsome man who takes pride in his masculinity. Memories still get the upper hand and push me over where I stand, like a nail in the earth, very wary. I have finally learned how to resist my longing. If I fell in love with him again, I would fall on my head, not on my feet. Forgetting would become impossible. Love would take up residence in my blood, I would become addicted to its presence there, and I would need a long period of recovery to rid myself of this addiction.

So I won't go back to him again.

Father with a Suspended Sentence

A man who looks like me, who was born in Gaza and didn't know any other city for a long time. For thirty years, he saw nothing but its north and south. He didn't know any city besides it. And now here he is, blending into another country.

Perhaps I am betraying Gaza through my presence outside it, in that I am free here while they suffer there. They suffocate under siege; it embarrasses me to enjoy my electricity day and night while they aspire to a few hours of lighting. This doesn't stop me from enjoying my recently recovered freedom. But my happiness is incomplete and my joy is temporary, and this freedom doesn't fulfill me anymore.

Here I was, boarding the tram in the streets of Antwerp. Boredom comes over me sometimes, so I kill it by exploring places I haven't seen yet. I ride the tram with no particular destination in mind, inviting it to lead me on an expedition to a place I haven't visited before. I let it do as it likes, and I shift my sights between the inside and the outside.

He was just dozing, on the seat reserved for children or the elderly. He looked very peaceful in his sleep, which made me wish I could lean his sleeping face on my shoulder. His neck was twisted so that a twinge of pain showed clearly on his face, while the depth of his sleep kept him from opening his eyes. I would have done it, placed his head on my shoulder, but I was afraid he would wake up and be scared to find a strange man getting close to him while he was unconscious—even if it was only to prop his head up so that he could sleep more comfortably.

I felt a need to belong to someone or to let someone belong to me.

Here he was opening his eyes, heavily, when the tram stopped to let on a girl with bronze skin and pretty eyes. Her cheekbones were on the high side, which added to the beauty of her features. She was wearing a blazer with long pants, without a trace of makeup on her face. She didn't need it, with her naturally radiant complexion. She seemed absorbed in serious thought. None of the riders paid attention to her beauty. The eyes of the women and the men turned instead to the girl who got on the tram wearing a short skirt, above her knees, and a shirt with thin straps that showed off the smoothness of her shoulders and the roundness of her chest. Her eyes weren't honey-colored or dark and neither was her hair; still, she piqued everyone's interest. But she didn't pique mine, because she didn't look like my city. She didn't look like my love. I was enthralled by this small, beautiful creature closing his eyes and falling back to sleep, because he reminded me of Gaza.

I heard two girls whispering about a boy who was standing by the back door, stealing glances at each of them in turn without showing any preference for one or the other. Or maybe he hadn't made up his mind yet about the girls' crush and their competition over him. I felt that I resembled him in his hesitation. My little one was still sleeping easily in his seat, paying no attention to either of the whispering girls or to the beautiful brown-haired girl who was kissing her boyfriend, their kiss untroubled by the commotion of the tram. They were weaving their worlds together, showing off their love, and I wondered, "Will their love last, or will they grow apart?"

My story with Gaza is a lot like their story. As much love as I shared with her, publicly and to this day, Gaza is still under punishment while I am free here. The name "Gaza" would suit a beautiful girl punished for the lust her God-given loveliness inspires. Accusations are thrown at her, and looks full of doubt and suspicion. And if her accusers realized their mistake, they might admit, "Some assumptions are sinful." I didn't realize until this moment how forgiving they had been with me and how harsh with her.

Almost every corner of the world was represented in the nationalities here. I could identify most of the languages spoken on the tram just by hearing them, even though I didn't understand the content of the conversations. Here, I have learned how to tell languages apart without understanding them—a skill that Brussels taught me, and later Antwerp.

This beautiful creature was shifting in his seat, and I could almost detect the fragrance of Gaza in his scent. An unfamiliar shiver of rapture came over me, drawing me into its consuming embrace. As for Baysan—she was a different story. I used to love listening to her speak. I was drawn to her Ghazzawi willfulness, one of the causes of death for our story.

When the tram stopped, two girls quietly speaking French got in. Antwerp is Flemish-speaking but prefers English for dealing with its visitors. One of the girls was blonde, and the other had dark hair. They were beautiful and mismatched. Their whispered conversation was interrupted by the ringing of a cell phone, which the dark-haired girl answered in her Moroccan dialect, "Right?! I'm not that 'open' for him to ask me. He should ask the Belgian girl—she might be down, if she's okay with having an Arab boyfriend." The word *open* was in English.

I didn't mean to laugh. I was like a crazy person, wanting to go up to her and ask her out in an effort to cheer her up. I wouldn't ask her for anything in return and wouldn't ask her to be "open" either; I was no longer tempted by young girls who fall in love easily. She would mature beyond her twenty years and would learn how silly she had been to cry over ruins whose landmarks would later disappear. And now here was my little one, opening his eyes; I wished I could get closer to him, enfold him in my arms, and stamp his face with a kiss. Why did he, specifically, bring on this emotional malaise in me? And why did I feel like he was related to me? Here he was, spraying the sea's mist in my face so that I could almost taste its salt in my mouth. Our eyes met for a few moments, but he didn't focus on me; I almost lost my mind. He had simply gone back to sleep. It was as if he were wearing Gaza, as if he were anointed with the fragrance of her harbor and perfumed with her earth. Why was he acting like he didn't know me? Was Gaza angry that I had reclaimed some of my freedom outside of her walls? This anger reminded me of Baysan's anger, which I didn't understand, whenever she decided to break up with me without even scolding me or giving our story the slightest chance. She would make this decision by herself, in her reckless stubbornness. I'm usually preoccupied when I get on the tram and don't look at any of the other passengers. I had decided today to observe what I had ignored before, and so I found Gaza here. And I started to notice things that I had gotten used to seeing, that had lost their foreignness and become part of my daily life.

Here was my little one, who looked like he might be around four, still in his slumber. Those same four years had passed without my seeing Baysan a single time. The motion of the engine rocked him. I was still unsettled by his innocence, which drew me toward him as if he were my own flesh and blood, as if some woman I had slept with in absentia had given birth to him and hidden him from me.

He's my child! He has the features of Gaza and the scent of Gaza and the pride of Palestine. He could practically be my child, whom Baysan kept from me with her distance. Why, woman, why did you hide my child from me?

I looked over at his mother, who I guessed was Hispanic based on her facial features, her bronze skin, and her prominent curves. She was pretty and had a nice figure. I tried to remember if she had ever slept in my bed. I racked my brain to find her there—this child had something of me in him!—but my memory betrayed me. I started to wonder: Had there ever been a Hispanic woman in my life?

This would have been our son if we hadn't split up, but splitting up was our fate. We tried but lost our love anyway. She ran away without leaving a single thread that could lead me back to her. She was hell-bent on separating, with her stupid hardheadedness.

The Hispanic woman was caught up in conversation with a woman in her sixties with beautiful pale blue eyes. The passage of years showed clearly on her face, but she had kept her beauty and the gleam in her eyes. She seemed very kind and was saying sweet things about my son, calling him a handsome boy. How could Gaza not be beautiful? It couldn't be any other way. It's a compound of divine beauty, the beauty of paradise mixed with the fire of Hell on Earth. That is the situation in Gaza.

The tram moved, and I was overwhelmed with the urge to take back the son who had been stolen from me for several years, during which time I had been deprived of my legal rights as his father. The other riders glanced covertly at the girl in her twenties with her hair flowing freely over her bare shoulders, while I peered furtively into my years of celibacy and tried to jam this child's mother into my life, as if I were inserting Gaza into my freedom.

I want her son to be my child, and I want him to be free.

The tram stopped again so that the "control" team could get on to check our tickets. Surprise campaigns that they undertake from time to time. It was only a matter of seconds until some young man tried to flee into the street, but luck was not on his side because the ticket-checkers flocked to arrest him, giving two other young men the opportunity to escape without anyone noticing. The poor guy started crying, hoping for compassion. Maybe he was living in Belgium illegally, and being arrested without papers would be catastrophic for him. Either prison or forced return to his country of origin. I lifted my head and my attention was momentarily captured by the scene in front of me. Then I looked down at the seat where Gaza had been sitting, in the form of a beautiful being. I couldn't find the boy; his mother had gotten off the tram without warning and kidnapped Gaza from me all over again. I still couldn't remember: When had his mother come into my bed? Maybe she had never come into it at all.

Fireworks

I sit on my green couch to welcome in 2015. I drink green tea alone, relaxed, in my element. The couch that's barely wide enough for two people. One of my plans for the New Year is to buy a bigger one in a feminine color. Maybe a pink or yellow couch, or maybe a bigger one with a neutral color this time to match my new living room, which has room for more visitors.

Two thousand fifteen will start with me in my new place. I feel entitled to steal a little happiness now, after living for a year and a half in a small studio where I was forced to host friends in the room where I slept and ate, which ceded more space day after day to my growing library. So don't be surprised by my delight in my new apartment, with its separate bedroom and living room and its 32-square-meter area. Having this kind of space is considered a feat in Brussels. As usual, I've gotten bogged down in details and forgotten why I started this story. I was talking about the New Year, which has come early, or maybe it's just that we used to forget to wait for it in the middle of the destruction plaguing us . . . but anyway.

I decided to welcome this year with extravagant laziness and turned down three invitations from friends to spend New Year's in their company. I felt an overpowering need for some calm and serenity. I won't lie to you, it was an eccentric choice, but I felt assured in it. I went to bed early in protest of the New Year's approach, which had always taken us by surprise and never brought a respite from our confusion and fear. This was my way of ignoring things. But this son of 60 bitches was determined.

At around 11:00 p.m., I woke up to the sound of fireworks going off. I tried to ignore them at first, but they got louder and forced me to get up.

I remembered standing in front of the window contemplating the far-off lights on one of the hot evenings in Gaza. Even though I was standing at the window on the tenth floor, I still wished for a breeze and invited it to tickle my cheek and my arms and neck. Its caress didn't stop the drop of sweat that was trickling down toward every part of my body. Despite the humidity, I enjoyed the nighttime calm and the beautiful view in front of me, where the houses were lined up side by side, embracing because they were stuck together so tightly. They were dimly lit, despite the randomly dispersed streetlamps. Even with many of the streetlights broken, Gaza looked beautiful.

It wasn't out of the ordinary for Gaza to wear this dark outfit—sometimes as funeral garb for the multitude of martyrs, sometimes because there wasn't enough diesel to fuel the manual electricity generator. It was routine for the power to go off, and we had gotten used to it then, to the point of missing the blackouts when the electricity dared to stay on for a whole day. We missed the clamor and the polluted dust. In Gaza, we had gotten used to the blockade . . .

Mish kalaam! How can I say that?

The sky lit up suddenly with bright colors, mixed and radiating light with a rumble that made my heartbeats vibrate along with it. "They're just fireworks." They felt like a trick, the beautiful prelude to an air raid; that was what I thought the first time I saw fireworks in Gaza. I remember them going off in abundance to send off the second millennium. These are just ghosts that drift through my memory, nothing more.

I kept sneaking peeks at what was happening. I was waiting for the end of the trick, for some house to blow up before my eyes. The noises stopped and the lights went out and then some leftover smoke floated up without any explosion.

"So they set off fireworks in Gaza too."

I pulled myself out of these memories and returned to my new reality: my street at the edge of the city, near the Brussels airport in Zaventem. The way people celebrate New Year's is wild here too. Usually these customs were limited to the city center, so I hadn't expected a small neighborhood to spend over half an hour ringing in the New Year with this much noise and carrying on.

I lifted my gaze to the sky. The plane disappeared. My Belgian neighbor in her fifties noticed my terror when a plane flew close by above us and asked me,

"What is it?"

"These planes circling above me bring back difficult memories."

"We've gotten used to the sound of planes circling here."

"When I hear them, my senses stop working. I'm always waiting for them to be followed by an explosion somewhere."

"Don't worry, these are safe planes."

"I know, but it's not easy to get rid of my fear. You can't blame me for that; I didn't have safe planes in my country to get used to."

"I suppose you always lose something in war . . ."

She doesn't know war, of course. She patted my shoulder, smiling, and then ambled into her house next door to mine. It's not that easy to shake off a habit of fear that has kept us company for many years.

The New Year had conspired with the neighborhood kids to ruin my peace tonight. I decided to go to them. I went down to the street in my pajamas, which I hadn't changed. I didn't wear a jacket to shield me from the biting cold outside. Maybe the memories hadn't left me so easily; every time fireworks went off near me, I shuddered as if they had activated something inside of me. I knew that these fireworks were just recreational, but in Gaza we don't have this luxury. These noises are linked in our memories to explosions and blood and martyrs. It's not easy to free ourselves from our memories, even though this is my eighth year in Belgium. I was born in Gaza while the war was going on, and lived years of my life there while the war was still going on, and will most likely die here as an immigrant without the war in Palestine having ended. I lived in Gaza as an immigrant and will die as an immigrant in Belgium. How many times I heard my grandfather's anecdotes and stories about his village, Baysan, when I was little. I was his favorite, even though there was hardly a single household in my extended family that didn't have a child named Baysan in it, at least in the first generation. I was named Baysan after the village, in honor of my grandfather's wish. Until his last breath, he still dreamed of going back. Sometimes I hate my name, which I love, because it reminds me that I've been displaced in my own country. My father has never been able to visit our village, but he loves it and dreams of returning to it. This love of his was transmitted to me. But life in Gaza is very hard, and immigrating to Belgium was the only solution.

The celebrations continued from midnight until dawn. My plans to go to sleep early so that I could wake up early, refreshed and ready for my appointment, had failed, and I had failed at not thinking too much this year. But it's not easy to shake off our habits. I wasn't ready to meet the New Year in my apartment, so it met me in the street.

Still, my plans for 2015 hadn't changed: buying a new couch and a new bed. Paying more attention to some friends I had neglected without meaning to and deleting some numbers I had no use for from my phone. And holding on to the wishes of last year.

Within two hours, movement and traffic would spread through the area; I had to decide if I was going to sleep a little or be two hours early for my appointment. I put on my black-and-white checkered dress. I don't know how I pulled it out of the closet after swearing never to wear it again; it was his gift to me for my 26th birthday. Why, on this particular day, did I feel ready for its softness to touch my body, when before it had felt like a needle pricking my skin? This dress prodded at my memory.

The Jealous Metro

I went into the metro station heading for the center of Brussels. I still had plenty of time before the evening, when I would attend an event for the Turkish writer Elif Shafak at the Bozar Centre for Fine Arts. I was coming from Antwerp just for this. A fear of nothing in particular was trying to get the better of me. A silence had come over the station, despite it being crowded with people. They walked quickly, not paying attention to their steps. I kept up with their speed even though there was no pressing task waiting for me at this moment. I got onto a metro car quickly, before the doors could shut in my face, and stood next to the door, barely seeing who was standing next to me because the car was so packed. The metro stopped at Place Sainte-Catherine, and I decided to get off and take a break from this stifling atmosphere. When the doors opened, I saw her approaching the metro car. I was sure. Her posture, which I had once loved. Her quick footsteps. And even the slight absent-minded movement of her head despite the business-like atmosphere around her. The black checkered dress that I loved on her—how often I told her that!

She got on through a different door, in a car parallel to mine. I was separated from her by a small partition. If I got off the metro I might lose track of her completely, so I got closer to the door separating our two cars once the train started moving on its way to the next stop, De Brouckère. She was hard to find in the throngs of people, but I finally spotted her, standing as if she were waiting for me. I don't know how she turned toward me and noticed me. Our eyes met. I was walking toward a question inside me that was becoming more insistent: Why had our separation stretched on so long? Why had I lost her the last time?

How many times we argued and then came back together to savor the sweetness of love, the way it had been in the beginning. How many times I started fights between us so that we could come back from them loving and longing for each other more. Right after our last fight, I lost all contact with her. Which one of us turned their back on our great love to run after delusions and mirages, her or me?

A void chases me that no woman could fill after you. My shadow mocks me by reminding me of the girls besides you who have knocked on the door of my life, some of whom did more than that. You were disappearing from me, little by little.

I forgot her, or at least that's what I thought.

You were far away from me, and I didn't bring you back into my love. I left you and let you master the game of separation while I let the curse of distance overtake us. For a while now, you've been peering out from my dreams. You look out of my mirror when I'm shaving my beard; out from my closet, where you pick out my clothes for me; and from the box of books, you remind me of the novels we argued about. The reason I've come here today is your love for this writer, whose books you were always pushing me to read. I hadn't even understood this covert dimension of my interest in the event until I saw you in front of me now, upright with pride, as usual.

Your sleepy voice still tickles my memories, reading to me from Elif Shafak's *The Forty Rules of Love*: "The lover who is nowhere to be found, you start to see everywhere. You see him in the drop of water that falls into the ocean, in the high tide that follows the waxing of the moon, or in the morning wind that spreads its fresh smell; you see him in the geomancy symbols in the sand, in the tiny particles of rock glittering under the sun, in the smile of a newborn baby, or in your throbbing vein."

I was living with you in every woman I knew after you; I was kissing them but was really kissing you. I missed you while they were in my arms. I would repeat your name when my desire cooled off, until I got caught repeating it once in a voice I thought only my body could hear. Your name left my lips, and the blonde woman sleeping next to me heard it. The spark of love in her eyes went out, but she didn't comment on it or ask me about you. The strange thing is that it was a relief for your name to leave my mouth, as if I had desperately needed to call out for you. To taste your name between my lips. I was hungry for you; I wished she would slap me or walk out. I felt a desire to talk about you to her. To tell her about us, about our fights and our stories and the kiss I stole from you by force, which put out fires inside of me that no woman who has come into my bed since has put out.

Could you have tasted that different from them?

Even my mirror reflected your face this morning, when I was surveying my features and saw yours. You were returning to occupy my imagination. And here you were now, returning to occupy my life—my imagination, infected with you for a long time, wasn't enough for you. I lifted my phone to ask for your number before I lost you again. You smiled in that way of yours that I know. You tried to form the numbers' shapes with your fingers, and despite the difficulty of this motion, you managed to get a few numbers across, and then the train stopped. I got off, with difficulty, to change cars and join you; I hadn't caught your full number, to call you and cut through the distance that sprawled out between us. I was almost to the door, standing in front of you without you noticing me, waiting my turn to get on.

You were standing in the car, leaning on the occupied seat next to you and looking for me in the car ahead with a longing that made me shiver. I wasn't used to seeing your face open with your emotions clearly on display, you who were so good at hiding them. When you left me and distanced yourself, you didn't leave a single thread behind to lead me to you. Had our chance meeting today softened your resolve?

How beautiful your unguarded face was!

How had my anger at you disappeared so completely? When had I forgiven you?

The metro betrayed me, issuing its warning that the doors were closing. The door snapped shut in my face and in the face of our return. I hadn't gotten your phone number; you could be waiting there for my return, not knowing how close I was, that I was standing next to you with only the metro door separating us. The metro started to move and got farther away, having snatched you away from me. It hadn't let me pierce through your weakness; maybe this was our beginning all over again.

I didn't run away in a rage like you might have thought. I had forgiven your long absence. It was the metro's fault, the jealous devil.

Muhammad Diab

Diary of a Depressed
Syrian in Germany

Translated by Graham Liddell

Translator's Reflection

The two-part personal essay that I have translated as "Diary of a Depressed Syrian in Germany" was originally published as two separate pieces on the Lebanese website *Al Modon*. The Arabic title of the first piece, which I have somewhat altered and applied to both of them collectively here, is *"Yawmiyyāt Mukta'ib Sūrī fī 'Almāniyā."* In this original title, the adjective and noun take positions opposite to those they take in my English rendering. The Arabic title translates more literally as "Diaries of a Syrian Depressive in Germany"; "Syrian" becomes a mere adjective to describe the fixed noun— "Depressive"—by which the author defines himself. Diab's narrativized version of himself, henceforth "the narrator," is not a Syrian who happens to be depressed, but rather a depressed person who happens to be Syrian.

The narrator seems at once hesitant to embrace Syrian as a category to which he belongs and deeply nostalgic for the homeland that he feels guilty for abandoning. On the one hand, he despises "trivial" discussions in which cultural heritage is "incessantly glorified and bragged about." The idea that members of the same ethnic group should essentially be alike is repulsive to him. On the other hand, his depression is deeply imbued with *al-ghurbah* in all senses of the word. *Al-ghurbah* is a place—"abroad, outside the Arab world"—but also an emotional experience—"alienation"—and a state of being— "strangerhood." Thus, the narrator's status as an outsider is always palpable to him.

Al-ghurbah manifests itself in the form of a lifestyle in which the narrator cordons himself off from others, at least emotionally. This isolation is in small part a reaction to his being made to feel unwelcome, especially in the face of a constant barrage of comments from Europeans about his beard. But his seclusion is largely intentional and self-imposed. It is a coping mechanism designed to prevent his wounds from being exposed and thus reopening. Of course, the narrator's isolation also comes at a cost: he forgoes the nourishment of close personal relationships that might be essential for his hidden wounds to heal.

In one of the essay's most poetic moments, the narrator gazes out the window at an old brick wall in the distance. It seems almost as if it has been transported to the modern city from a bygone era. Its natural wear and haphazard appearance reminds him of his hometown in Syria, and its out-of-placeness reminds him of himself. Its very purpose as a wall is to separate and protect, just as the narrator hopes to keep his true feelings and thoughts set apart from his interactions with others.

By the end of the second part of the essay, this solitude shows its true colors: profound loneliness. The narrator finds himself craving human connection, despite the intensity of his judgmental attitude toward nearly everyone he encounters. The truth, he admits, is that he finds beauty in his negative thoughts, in their unabashed and naked truth. What if he could find beauty somewhere else—perhaps in another human being who was his equal in strangerhood? Perhaps the ensuing relationship would instill a craving for mutual care in place of his addiction to (self-)judgment.

Diary of a Depressed Syrian in Germany

Part I

In the silence of the depressed, there is something of the silence of death. When a depressed person keeps his distance from you, do not assume it is because he hates you. He who is depressed is incapable of hating, of wasting his emotional energy on violent feelings. He is angry, but his anger is silent and concealed. It is not others, primarily, at whom he is angry, but himself. He directs his anger back toward himself, and it convulses deep within him, down to the roots. He becomes distressed and burdened. Words, time, people, responsibilities, simple everyday tasks, even basic movement—all of these weigh him down.

The depressed person may not have the strength to prepare his own food, even when hunger bites. He may neglect to bathe and fail to change his sheets. Despite understanding the necessity of doing these things, he surrenders to distress and discontent, to the overwhelming desire to cry, or . . . to suicide.

In the past few weeks, I have completely separated myself from social media platforms, preferring to keep what I write to myself. I have gone back to writing on paper. I have been writing as prolifically as I used to—perhaps even more. Since I started writing, my aim has never been to publish my work. I like others to read my thoughts, and I know that usually, my writing is about things that remain buried in people's souls for their entire lives. But I don't like the true intentions of my writing to be understood. I despise narrow-mindedness, prejudices, empty jargon, lack of imagination, and stupid interpretations. That's why I stopped using social media.

I have always considered writing my only way to expel depression and restlessness from my chest, even if inadequately. But I have found that writing online, and all the silly and ridiculous judgments that spring from cyberspace onto whomever the writer may be, results in a great deal of fatigue, stress, depression, and sometimes regret.

I try to push away these negative, overwhelming feelings, to live life the way it was in the 1990s, which I much preferred to nowadays. I have long wished that the flow of time had stopped there forever, that the hands of the clock had broken at the end-of-the-century marker. I almost never reach for my cell phone except to answer very routine, work-related calls. I try to maintain a balanced daily schedule to make this life as tolerable as possible.

✦ ✦ ✦

I get out of bed in the morning. I smoke a few cigarettes. I shower in lukewarm water. I brush my teeth. I trim my beard, because I can barely stand opposite a European without him or her talking about it, using the same tedious phrases. My beard still arouses suspicion, anxiety, and doubt in these cold, intolerant societies, which boast of openness and glorify personal freedoms at every possible occasion. I put on my clothes. I prepare my morning coffee. I finish it quickly with several cigarettes. I proceed on my way to my class, which is preparing me for a particular line of work. I spend approximately a third of my day there. I very rarely speak to anyone. Among the things I try to practice: destroying my ego completely, refraining from speaking to anyone about my personal thoughts, curtailing my ever-present anger by concealing it.

I know my thoughts are very critical and harsh. My mood is melancholic and tense to the point of illness. My tastes are almost impossible to satisfy. And the criteria of my judgments are immune to being tricked by appearances, whether of people or their actions.

I no longer show enthusiasm or emotional excitement. I don't talk about my personal life or my feelings about the outside world. I try to make do with casual, shallow conversation, often resorting to gestures to spare myself from speech.

I think that in the past I expended an enormous amount of energy, and to no avail whatsoever. Now I am completely resigned to a fact that has become clear to me: nothing is changeable. I have taken great pains, exerted many emotions, and sickened my heart and my nerves to explain and express and critique and discuss. Perhaps I have taken that too far. So here I am, killing my old habits one by one, as if destroying stones in some video game. I have become so drained and discontented that I can no longer maintain those habits.

In the classroom on the first floor, I sit near a window that looks out at some residential buildings that have a classical architectural style. Their walls stand erect, dividing the university from a residential neighborhood. I am dogged by the habit of letting my attention drift, recollecting the memories of my childhood there, in that country that I left. Suddenly, without my willing it, the memories attack my mind. I try to keep them under control, to focus on the lecture about the complicated laws in the constitutions of European Union countries, laws that create links between individual citizens, between the state and the citizen, and between the states of the Union.

In my distractedness I spend a long time contemplating those ordinary walls. Simple cement building blocks with bricks on top. Neglected soil gathering at the bottom, a result of time and wind. That moss that has the ability to grow on stone. Lines extending in many directions on one of the walls. Perhaps they were left behind by an old, now-uprooted tree that used to grow vines on that wall, tracing the way to an abandoned shop.

Absent-mindedly, I reflect on these things and am overwhelmed by grim, violent emotions that seem like a kind of nostalgia. They twist around my body and legs like the arms of an octopus, pulling me down to the darkness of the bottomless depths, where I drown. I suffocate and my body fills with salt water, then floats to the surface. Alone on the horizon, a roaring wave hurls it in the air.

This is what happens when the late-May sun bestows a tinge of age-old anguish onto the wall in the noonday calm. The wall seems out of place in this highly regulated section of a European city, like a dancer on a tightrope—at a funeral. The scene reminds me of Syria, of my coastal city, Latakia, in the land I left behind. That "good earth" that I love. The simple neighborhoods where I was brought up. The narrow streets. The random buildings tarnished by the smoke of car exhaust. The school I attended in childhood and adolescence.

✦ ✦ ✦

During the break I go out and drink a cup of coffee or two from the automatic machine. With my coffee I smoke a few cigarettes in the designated smoking area. At my side are a few smokers from my class. We exchange chatter, sometimes complaining about the instructor's poor teaching style, which I find rigid and idiotic, like that of an old Soviet army officer. But I keep that particular opinion to myself rather than sharing it with my classmates.

I do not go with them to fast food restaurants near the university. I never eat meals like that. Alone in my room, I prepare my food in the evenings. For years, without any compelling reason, I have committed to a healthy diet that some might find austere. But I no longer see it that way. Rather, I have come to live a lifestyle that fits the type of exercise I have been doing since childhood.

I leave the group and return to the study hall. From my bag I take out something I prepared last night. I go to the kitchen on the upper floor. I heat my food in one of the microwaves lined up in a row on a slab of marble. I eat with students from different classes. None of us knows one another, so no conversation passes between us. I finish my food. I wash my lunchbox made of safe-use plastic. I wash my hands. I smoke a cigarette. I return to the hall. I take my place. I pull some novel out of my bag. With my back to the door and my face to the window, that wall stands directly across from me. That wall for which a strange sentimentality has emerged in my soul. And now an even stranger relationship is beginning to form between us. I sink in my seat. I read from my book as the lunch break comes to a close, waiting for the return of the remaining students and the loathsome instructor.

The final hours of class time tick away slowly. But they eventually pass.

I return to my apartment, change my clothes, and go to the gym. I stay there for approximately two hours, immersed in my daily exercises. I try to exhaust my body to the greatest extent possible in order to be able to sleep at night. This has been my method to win a years-long fight against insomnia. Exercise is the cornerstone of my strict daily routine, which keeps me at a distance from depression, even though this distance is unsafe and purely imaginary.

I finish my workout and go grocery shopping. I return to my

room. I shower in lukewarm water. I put my clothes in the washing machine. I cook enough meals to last me a week. Four varieties of meals. As I wait for the food to cook, I wash the pots and dishes. I straighten up the room. I eat a light meal. I wash the dishes again. I strive to keep everything in its right place, since clutter can afflict me with distress. I review the new information that came up in class. I take an antidepressant, and I end my day by writing or reading while listening to music. Or I fall asleep watching a Spanish or French film.

✦ ✦ ✦

Despite my buried feelings, I believe that the way I have structured my life is not only healthy, but positive. It keeps me from a wearisome addiction to wasting time on social media websites, an epidemic that has ravished multitudes on this planet. My grades on the initial practice exams in general education have been good, even though I am the sole foreigner in a group of EU citizens.

I behave formally and courteously with people, despite my aversion to formalities, which I merely act out and wear as a mask in order to create distance between myself and others. I only speak with them when necessary. When I'm asked a question, I answer concisely, without commentary or elaboration.

In our cohort, students are descended from various cultures, and there is often talk of people's customs and the ways they differ. I despise these trivial and irritating conversations, in which *belonging* is incessantly glorified and bragged about. The only virtue of these conversations is that they immediately reveal the level of intelligence or stupidity of the speaker. I laugh when they laugh, and I ask questions as they do if I don't understand some idea clearly. But before long I stop talking, since I recognize that conversations like these consist only, for the most part, of surface-level naïveté and platitudes.

I put an enormous amount of energy into seeming like a normal person, to the extent that is possible. But the immense effort I exert to hide my personal feelings, to compel myself to engage with real life, goes to waste.

On the last day of class last week, the instructor approached me alone in the study hall during the break and asked if I was suffering from some kind of depression or mental disorder. His question caught me off guard, and I felt a cold tingling flow throughout my entire body. Managing to regain my composure and conceal what came over me, I held up my book, painted a phony smile on my face, and responded: "No, not at all! It's just that this novel's depressing vibes have rubbed off on me, but they're just fleeting feelings." A moment later I darted out of the hall, pretending to take a phone call.

✦ ✦ ✦

And now I am thinking: depression is like a scar left by a wound on someone's face. A wound that time cannot erase and that surgery cannot repair, no matter how skilled the doctor. It remains distinct and indelible in the features of depressed people, even the densest of simpletons among them.

The instructor's question overwhelmed me with alarmingly destructive emotions, ruining what I had earnestly sought to create in the past few weeks. They are like the emotions of a child who spends all day building a sand castle on the beach, and no sooner does he finish and gaze upon it in wonder than, in a single instant, it comes crashing down under the stomping foot of a bully passing by on the seashore.

Part II

Pain shocks you, shakes you to your core. It makes you purer on the inside, in the depths of your soul, and makes you more perceptive of others. Pain awakens your consciousness, and you reconsider things you used to believe in. It pushes you to be more honest with yourself, to become more resilient. To be smarter in your dealings with those you pity, so you won't be deceived so easily, the way you were in the past.

But none of this lasts.

How agonizing it is to live in the turmoil of excessively exploring people's cavernous inner worlds. Of recognizing their motivations and yours, along with the fact that life is absurd and humiliating, and everything in it is a mere wisp of smoke. A person can never learn to live with such a mischievous, suffering consciousness, no matter how much it has hardened his heart.

Deep loneliness is the fate of wandering souls. Discerning eyes see further than they should. People who indulge in thinking and feeling more than necessary can be totally destroyed by the harsh, inescapable truth.

You wish you hadn't plumbed the dark, miserable depths—those that display the world, the words and deeds of humankind, all the more clearly in that darkness. You wish you weren't aware of those intentions, that you were incapable of uncovering the real hidden beneath the counterfeit. In fact, you wish there were no such thing as real or counterfeit but that the two were one and the same. You wish you could continue on in self-delusion, not thinking, not feeling, not remembering.

But you have to submerge yourself in the darkness of painful truths once in a while. Until, inevitably, you are deceived, and you begin to believe and trust and quit doubting yourself and others. You start trusting in them, in life, in yourself. You start believing in something. That you are a hero in one of their stories.

But no matter what you do or how hard you try, you'll never reclaim what pain took away from you, never rid yourself of what it introduced you to. There's absolutely no way to get something back when it was just an illusion in the first place. Is there?

Wouldn't it have been better to remain naïve, an oblivious spectator applauding with the masses?

But you've left the herd and won't be able to return to it.

What have you accomplished with all this thinking of yours, in the end? Philosophy? Writing? You are becoming a farce, a ridiculous joke that everyone loves to crack together. You've walked yourself into the abyss on your own two feet.

So to hell with reason, then. Right? Reason leads only to one place. A place where the world and everything in it are thrown into sharp, horrifying relief—and to no purpose. A place where life's naked facts are on full display. The fact that life is a shackle that makes reasonable people miserable, and all they want is to be freed from it. The fact that living is an endless succession of struggles and pains.

You start to regret every time you've opened your heart to others and spoken to them sincerely about yourself—about your thoughts, your past and your fantasies, your desires and your suffering.

You regret, no matter how much it had seemed to you that you wouldn't regret. It is best, therefore, upon feeling a sense of compatibility with some person, to choose cautiously and carefully what you share with him or her—what you express, driven by a sentimental impulse. To choose to share something that won't make you regretful for an extended period of time. Something that won't make you feel bitter or revolted, like you gushed too much to the person, especially since he or she will soon become a stranger to you. You'll both become strangers to one another, the way you were before you met.

There's no reason to feel bitter about the fact that you're naïve enough to fall in love with one of these people. There is nothing wrong or harmful in that. For this is the type of naïveté that eases the pain of life, just as deviance does. Love may be nothing but a type of deviance. But you always have to be cautious, even fearful, of getting so attached to someone that you accept becoming idiotic and pathetic.

✦ ✦ ✦

I hate truisms. I hate the millions of people who are deeply in love with intellectual truisms. It is an absolute aversion, an utter disgust, that I have for truisms and their millions of adherents. They quite literally make me sick.

The myriad truisms that the Facebookites persist in typing up and posting have achieved a popularity that has helped turn basic romantics into celebrities, bolstering their delusions that they are geniuses, great authors, philosophers. A herd-mentality fame—such is the fame of Facebook's "poets."

It would make the world a lot better if we refrained from applying general, overarching standards for beauty. If we accepted the idea that some individuals among us are different from others in style, appearance, forms of expression, and mentality.

I just woke up after dozing off for a few minutes. While I was asleep, I had a strange dream that couldn't have lasted more than seconds. A dream light and sweet like the morning nap in which it visited me. I saw myself in that dream, sitting at my desk in the theater where I work.

It was a summer afternoon and the weather was calm. The sun was in the middle of the sky, and its light came down through the window behind me, extending its rays onto my back and my hair. With a wandering gaze, I looked out through the window at it, then down at the river, the bridge, and the trees to my right. At pedestrians and at children playing on the short grass that has become a napping site for addicts and vagrants. All the days of the summer they gather there, smoking hashish and sleeping on the grass with their dogs.

And there is the humble café on the bank of the river. A café that serves its cheerful patrons cold beer and basic snacks. Absent-mindedly, I observe these scenes from the window, scenes that alert me to the loneliness I've felt all these years I've lived here in Germany. As I am immersed in my roving thoughts, the sun from the window consoles me, caressing my arm and my beard. From the entrance of the theater opposite me, the warm sun sneaks in and casts its light upon my cold chest.

Yes, my chest is cold, haunted as it has been for years by the insecurity planted in my eyes, whose light has been extinguished by my indulgent loneliness.

✦ ✦ ✦

No sooner had you entered the theater than suddenly the heart-rending silence of my loneliness shattered and dissipated in the clatter of your footsteps and in your smile. Your ever-present smile that you show while your lips move to begin speaking, while you look at people's faces . . .

You came into my office, and, as usual, you patted yourself on your own shoulders with a tragicomic smile, a sign for a hug, which the current circumstances have forced us to avoid. You were beautiful as usual, and I was delighted to see you, happy to be in your presence. But we are strangers, just two colleagues who happen to work in one place. Maybe I've lost my emotional ability to take the initiative. I have no idea whether this interest is coming from one side or two.

I had told you the night before that I would soon be moving to work somewhere else. That upset you, and you said, "No, please stay here! I'd be sad if you left." Did you really mean that, or were you simply expressing a general, neutral kindness that is required by casual politeness when a colleague departs? I don't know. I could be mistaken. But from your eyes and the way you look at me when you're passing by and those simple conversations we have, the longest of which don't last more than five minutes or so, I have felt that you were interested in me.

But as you see, I may be mistaken. That's how I always am, immersed in my own world, in its details and in analyzing them: this world, where I am a complete stranger; that faraway world, from which I departed and distanced myself . . . I've become a stranger to that world, too, here in this cold country.

Has life—your life—ever deprived you of the emotional strength necessary to take the initiative and express your interest and your desire to get close to someone? I hope this hasn't afflicted you as it has me. I know how much this avoidance can trouble one's heart, one's life. I know how dreadful it can be.

Perhaps it is strange for you to be reading this letter of mine now. For me to be suddenly talking to you in this way about my feelings. For me to have developed such deep feelings for you in the first place, when we've only gotten to know each other the way a stranger gets to know another "stranger in a strange land" like him.

In these few months that we've known each other, whenever I noticed you passing by, whenever our eyes met in the theater, or while we were walking through hallways or between offices, for a moment I forgot what it was that was weighing on my mind.

In my short dream, you came into my office wearing a simple country dress. You were on your way to the makeup and costume room to prepare for the next theater performance. After our socially distanced embrace, in accordance with the preventative procedures of the pandemic, and after you smiled a sad, subtle smile, and after we chatted for a few minutes, you said, "Oh, I almost forgot." And suddenly you bent your head over your shoulder and pulled something from your ear, then from your other ear, and you put your earrings in my hand. You continued, "I'll leave them with you now and come get them at the end of the performance. Is that alright?"

With childlike happiness, I replied, "Of course, of course. As a matter of fact, I can keep them with me always."

At that particular moment, I felt emboldened and let my guard down. I loosened my grasp and looked at the two earrings. They were simple and sparkling, and in the center of each of them was a small stone that was the exact blue of the sky. I brought my hand to my face and smelled the earrings, your scent. In this position, in your presence, before your eyes, to which I hadn't yet lifted my gaze . . . the dream came to an abrupt end. And before I awoke, a few words of yours, pronounced in your delicate tone, reached my ears: "What are you doing, you crazy man?"

Unfortunately, I was not able to look at you after that to gauge your reaction to my behavior. In my dream, I hadn't been able to let that behavior remain a fantasy, and it escaped me despite myself. Could I find out your reaction now, if I told you, "I want to be immersed in you, and in your things, the way I was in my dream"?

What do you say, O familiar stranger close to my heart, you whose beauty is the beauty of pain?

Mohamad Alasfar

From *Dates and Wild Artichokes*

Translated by James Vizthum

Translator's Reflection

Even though the following excerpt comprises only the first few chapters of Mohamad Alasfar's novel *Dates and Wild Artichokes*, it tells a story in and of itself. The reader is introduced to a narrator who is obsessed with eating dates from his home country of Libya in his neighborhood in his country of refuge, Germany. The narrator's perpetual habit of eating Libyan dates and discarding the pits develops into a delightful tale with some unexpected and exciting twists. However, on top of this lighthearted narrative that captures the reader's attention, the author simultaneously presents the deeper, emotionally challenging aspects of living in refuge, both through the narrator's direct statements and memories and through numerous metaphors interspersed throughout the story.

The excerpt also makes a somewhat respectful mockery of German society. In one scene—the investigation into the missing date pits—the reader witnesses the order and efficiency of the fictional German municipality to an almost comical degree. This scene also reveals a subversive element: a lowly refugee is able to manipulate this system, even if his goal is something as seemingly insignificant as disposing of date pits on the grass. However, the tossing of date pits here may represent the figurative notion of planting a small seed that leads to great changes. At one point in the excerpt, the narrator frankly declares that "dates, as far as I am concerned, are a red line." This succinct statement ties together the story being told and the underlying theme of refugee life. For each refugee, there is a red line: a part of him or her that will always be tied to another culture and country, which no amount of time and acclimation will ever erase. By insisting that he maintain one specific aspect of his identity (tossing date pits on the grass), the narrator eventually succeeds in transforming the society around him. In other words, while the Germans have graciously accepted him as a "guest" in their society, in the end, both sides change each other.

From the perspective of translation, the novel presents two unique challenges. First, the author uses colloquial Libyan phrases to emphasize the narrator's specific identity. When translating these phrases into English, the underlying point of choosing those specific phrases may be lost. For example, the narrator sings a delightful song while eating Libyan dates. However, simply translating the lyrics into English would eliminate any indication that the song is Libyan. To make these instances clear, I have provided transliterations of the Arabic immediately ahead of English renderings of colloquial phrases and song lyrics. Finally, the title of the novel, *Tamr wa-Qa'mūl*, also poses a translation challenge. While "dates" is straightforward, the second word is not. *Qa'mūl* is a plant that only grows in one specific region of Libya, and efforts to find a unique translation for this word proved unsuccessful. The plant is, however, a type of wild artichoke, which thus enables the title *Dates and Wild Artichokes*. Perhaps this title, like the refugee in the story, can only assimilate to another language to a certain degree, with one aspect maintaining a distinct Libyan identity.

From *Dates and Wild Artichokes*

Dates

When I eat an orange, I keep the peel in my hand until I find a garbage can and throw it away. When eating dates, however, I don't look for a garbage can; I toss the pit directly on the grass. I never throw the pit on the asphalt for fear that cars will crush it.

I don't pay attention to the glances of disapproval at my actions, but rather I make excuses for these people, saying to myself that they are German citizens, and they can protest my actions if they want. After all, it is their country, and I am merely a temporary refugee. They graciously welcomed me and offered assistance, and I must respect their hospitality. Therefore, I shouldn't toss date pits in their parks but rather place them in spaces designated by the municipality for refuse, spaces every forty or fifty meters that have trash cans lined with plastic bags that municipal employees change two or three times a day.

I like to toss the pits on the soil. The sweetness of the date on my tongue orders me to do so. My heart requests that I sing:

Mawj an-nakhl khatar ʿalayya bilaadi
ya raytni wallayt minni ghaadi

The wave of the date palm brings my country to mind
how I wish I could return

I love the date palm. I see it as a graceful plant, lighthearted, its leaves like arms that wrap around me, and its date in my mouth that dances and sings. Unfortunately, I have not found a date palm in my place of refuge. I have found tall things, short things, and beautiful things, but not a date palm. I must, therefore, find my date palm in my own way. To me, each date is a palm oasis, and each palm oasis is home.

Since arriving in Germany, I have bought Libyan dates from a Moroccan or Iraqi grocery store, but when I do not find my favorite brand of dates at these places, I request them from Libya. They come to me with the next Libyan traveling for medical care. I wish the sick a speedy recovery, and if they need help, I gladly offer it. Then I receive the precious treasure of my country. The type of date — *Tabuni, 'Ami, Deglet, Saidi, Bikrari, Mirwani, Khadrawi, Barni, Negmet, Halawi,* etc. — is not a problem for me. All Libyan dates, in my opinion, are delicious; my sense of taste welcomes them, and I become overjoyed.

The German market offers excellent dates from a number of African Arab and Asian countries. Their price is low, but I don't buy them because they do nothing for me. These dates would not bring me joy even if they were stuffed with gold or dollars rather than just almonds or pistachios. The date must be the Libyan date that I know intimately — its flavor delighting my spirit — with dust covering it as if to preserve my happiness. When I blow on the dates, the dust scatters far, and the dates emerge like a sunrise greeting me, saying, "Welcome, my fellow countryman." And before my throat can burst into song, the dates beat me to it, singing:

Shabah an-nakhl khatar 'alayya bilaadi
The sight of the date palms brings my country to mind

The dates sing this song to me, set to the music of their palm leaves as the warm winds rock them back and forth, specifically the *qibli* winds of Libya — the warm southern winds carrying dust. Folk musicians sing of these winds:

Wa-yaa shaynak qibli sarhaadi
Haazak ya ghazayyel fil-waadi

Oh, what an awful, burning qibli wind
It stopped you in your tracks, O gazelle in the valley

The song "The Sight of the Date Palm Brings My Country to Mind" does not, unfortunately, come to me with the dates from other countries, dates I see and taste without any particular frame of mind. Algerian dates are delicious, Iraqi dates please me, Tunisian dates bring me joy, and Gulf dates aren't bad, but Libyan dates are unmatched and unrivaled. The song only stirs in my soul when accompanied by Libyan dates. I have become accustomed to their taste, their feel. Perhaps I have truly become addicted to Libyan dates. When I am without them even for a short time, a million jinn and 60 million devils pursue me. I become anxious, I get headaches and a fever, and my liver hemorrhages.

The family doctor is a dark-skinned woman of Moroccan descent who helps me quickly with a fresh smile. The smile looks like the cloven date that is dripping with honey, so I calm down a little bit. And in order to be friendly and do justice by her magical smile, I calm down a lot—even entirely. She says to me, "Sit in the chair and relax . . . Imagine yourself at Cafe Hafa in Tangier sipping on mint tea."

I say to her, "I'm there now, and I'd be lying to you if I told you I'm imagining it."

The doctor analyzes my blood and urine, takes my pulse, and measures my blood pressure and sugar levels. Then, she tells me, "The analysis is normal, you are healthy." I feel her whisper to me, "Sing your song about dates and you will improve. Sing until your country's dates come to you. Singing about one's homeland is, in and of itself, a blessed medicine from God. Have you sent an email for an urgent shipment of your beloved Libyan dates? If you haven't done so, don't delay any longer, my friend. I can write you a prescription with just one word: *dates*."

I respond to her whispers: "I have emailed more than once, Doctor, but the Libyan representative said, 'We do not ship the dates.' However, I must, somehow, get my special dates. In the meantime, I'll keep eating any Libyan date I can get, and I'll keep tossing the pits here and there. Perhaps one dear pit—*bint halal*—will be kind enough to sprout, giving me the sweetness of my homeland that I need."

Apartment

The distance between the apartment in which I live with my family and the bus stop from which I take a bus downtown every day is around 150 meters. The road to the bus stop is surrounded by green areas and small parks attached to buildings. To the right of my apartment is a Protestant church that has dark-skinned nuns. To the left of my apartment is a Catholic church that has white-skinned nuns. I don't differentiate between the two groups of nuns, just as I don't differentiate between the crosses of the two churches, or between the ringing of their noisy bells.

In front of our residential building is a supermarket and a number of other places offering goods or services: a pharmacy . . . a women's stylist . . . a café . . . a restaurant . . . a tailor . . . a dry cleaner . . . a perfume store . . . a post office . . . a bakery . . . a small bank . . . a dental clinic . . . a sports center. Behind our residential building there is a nursing home and beside it a private international school for the well-to-do. The curriculum at the school is in English, and the tuition is exorbitant. Behind the private school is a public elementary school where German students from blue-collar homes study with children of immigrants. There is also a kindergarten connected to the back of the Catholic church, and not far from that is a small police outpost inside of a ground-floor apartment in a tall residential building. The police outpost is closed. A policewoman only comes when there is work to do or a problem. She is a beautiful policewoman with blonde braided hair and a body that is tall, well-built, and athletic. Her hat passes in the window, and in her left nostril there is a thin, silver ring. And the middle of her right cheek—*ya saatir!*—is adorned with a lovely brown mole.

I really like seeing the policewoman as she walks elegantly toward the police outpost. A woman's walk excites me more than her face. A woman's gait has a special beauty, a beauty that makes my heart dance. Some steps smile. Some steps laugh. Some steps scowl. Some steps welcome you. Some steps flee from you. Some steps entice you. Some steps are barefoot. Some steps wear sandals. Some steps make the hips shake, going up and down and rotating along the way; one hip insults and another hip curses. Some steps do whatever they like. Ah, the footsteps, just the steps alone!

Once, I lost my ID card and informed the policewoman at the outpost. She made a report and said, "We will call you if we find it." When they found it at the supermarket in a nearby neighborhood—I had dropped it when paying for groceries—she brought it right to the door of my apartment. She requested that I sign a proof of receipt on a small device with an electronic screen. I signed and then invited her to have tea or coffee or a martini, but she apologized for not having time, since she had to follow up with other important issues. In that case, I said, we should take a selfie to mark the occasion of finding the ID card. She happily agreed. We took the picture and I thanked her profusely, telling her, "The police in your country are really in service of the people."

She responded, "And also in service of our refugee brothers and sisters, whom we look forward to seeing assimilated into our society and becoming part of our people."

I really like to see her, but unfortunately infractions and security problems in our neighborhood are few, and she is barely present. Violations would need to occur for me to see her jumping out of her car and running toward the offenders, handcuffs, pistol, and electric baton swinging around her waist as if in an action movie. I get pleasure from observing expressions on her face other than those of joy and love for the job. Perhaps I will commit an infraction myself—something simple that I am guaranteed to get out of scot-free. A gentle, sweet infraction that is not harmful to anyone else—or to me, of course.

Our housing complex was constructed in 1966, but it is still as good as new, as if it were built only five years ago. Perhaps the building was maintained in such good condition because of the civilized residents who lived in it before us, or maybe it is due to regular maintenance operations undertaken by the company that owns it. On a daily basis, a representative of the company passes by the buildings and records observations that can even include a dirty stairwell. In that case, the next day, the company sends you a warning letter claiming that if the stairwell is not cleaned within a week, *dear esteemed resident*, "we will pay for a cleaning company to clean it, and we will transfer the bill to you for mandatory payment."

Living is comfortable in the housing complex, and no one suffers from any deficiencies related to electricity, water, telephone, internet, heating, or any other household necessity. All of the residents in the neighborhood are happy, and no one mentions any problems, quarrels, or disputes. There are no complaints of trash in the stairwell or by the main door, and no complaints of dirt or smears on the window glass. Even the fallen leaves, as soon as someone gathers them into a small pile, are collected by being sucked into a wide, metallic scoop.

Most of the neighborhood residents are Germans, along with immigrants from various nationalities: Albanians . . . Serbians . . . Montenegrins . . . Kosovans . . . Georgians . . . Russians . . . Syrians . . . Moroccans . . . people from the Horn of Africa . . . Yemenis . . . people from Central and Western Africa . . . Iranians . . . Afghans . . . Cubans, Venezuelans, and other Latinos. As for Libyans, we are it. There was a small number of Libyan families that came to study at the expense of the Libyan government. However, we were unable to get to know them in a deep or satisfactory way, and all of those relationships were merely superficial. Those families were not families of the Cyrenaica cities (*Barqah*, or the eastern region of Libya). We can enter their hearts with a smile, with the folk poetry of *ghanaawah 'alam*, or with the expression *liman bil-jawda?*—"To which great tribe do you belong?" Or, "Greetings to my kin! You're our uncles or brothers-in-law"—*kheekhi wa-bin 'eekhi*, as we say. But these families are from other cities in western Libya, and our relationship with them—despite our proximity in the neighborhood—is quite limited. If we happen to meet at a bus stop, metro station, market, or the mosque for Friday prayers or religious holidays, we are confined to simple greetings such as "Peace be upon you . . . How are you doing?"

Squirrels

Before leaving the apartment, I put a handful of the dates I enjoy in my pocket, and I toss the pits on the green surfaces close to our building and along the way to the bus stop. As usual, I see the silent glances of disapproval on the faces of the Germans, and, of course, I don't pay any attention. The people standing in front of the two churches are good and tolerant; not one of them has ever scolded or reprimanded me. Martin Luther, God rest his soul—there are no problems between him and me. Nor between me and the Vatican

Pope, may God grant him long life. I pass by, tossing the pits, and I don't face actual harm from the Christians, merely friendly glances of protest which strike me as reprimand, but I pay no heed to those piercing rebukes. Dates, as far as I am concerned, are a red line. Simply put, when I chew these dates and enjoy their sweetness at my leisure, and afterward toss their pits into the womb of life, I barely notice anyone else. In those moments, my delight bursts into Arabic song . . . *Seeing the date palm brings my country to mind.*

Despite my persistence in my beloved daily ritual, no one had reported me to the local authorities. And as for any date pit that I toss on the ground on any given day, I never see it the day after. It simply disappears from the place where I had tossed it, and I don't know who picks it up from the green spaces. Perhaps it is the street sweeper that passes each morning to clean the streets, sucking up cigarettes and leaves. However, that vehicle does not go up onto the green surfaces—all of its work is on the paved road or sidewalk. Whatever the case may be, my routine with the date pits did not continue in this manner, as one evening I returned home and, before going up to my apartment, I checked the mailbox and found—oh shit! *Hayih 'ala imik ya layd!*—a letter from the municipality. The letter notified me of an urgent summons to investigate my continued littering on a public street. They specified a day and time to stand before them with a warning for failure to appear.

At city hall, they showed me a number of pictures of myself tossing the date pits. In truth, I had no intention of denying this or of seeking legal counsel to defend me. Rather, I was happy to immediately confess to tossing the pits on the fertile German soil and to admit doing so willfully and wholeheartedly. The investigator, with a thin, blond mustache said, "Someone observed your behavior, brought pictures to us, and we, in our role, would like to know why you are doing this and doing this regularly." He added, adjusting his glasses with his thumb and index finger, "The fact that you continue to throw the pits on the ground is something that we cannot ignore, and we had considered the issue to be a psychological condition or illness that requires early treatment. We do not consider this to be a mere coincidence or a joke that you will cease doing after you have gotten your fill."

I nodded my head in agreement, and he added, "Don't worry about this summons. We mainly want to help you, as you are a guest in our country, and throughout your stay with us you have respected all of the laws, and no violations or infractions have been recorded. You can respond now, or you can wait until you call a doctor, lawyer, or a sworn interpreter. All of your rights are guaranteed, and your dignity is safeguarded by the German constitution."

I said to him, "I toss the date pits out in the open, and all of the Germans in my area watch me with their own eyes and not one of them requested that I stop doing this. Every day I toss five or seven pits and they never pile up anywhere."

The investigator said, "You are right that there aren't any piles of date pits. After receiving the photographs, we went there more than once, and we swept the area with our equipment, and, unfortunately, we didn't find any pits on the ground. However, the pictures and video clips make it clear that you were indeed tossing the pits on the ground."

I glanced at the pictures to find out from which corner or location I had been photographed. From the church? No. From the market or other businesses? No. It had to be from an apartment window of the building adjacent to ours, one with no tall trees in front of it that would block the photographer's view. Who exactly is this do-gooder who was observing me? If only I knew, I could say thank-you in my own way.

The investigator said, "We investigated the matter and discovered that the pits you were throwing are being gathered by the many squirrels spread throughout your mountainous neighborhood. Your neighborhood was originally a dense forest before part of it was cleared to build residences in the 1970s. One day, we were observing you from a position where you couldn't see us, and we saw a squirrel, whose color was somewhere between yellow and brown, take a pit that you had tossed behind you while you were smiling. Then the squirrel quickly climbed the trunk of a tall tree with the pit. Here is a picture of the squirrel."

I looked at the picture, and there really was a gold-colored squirrel, one that I had seen more than once scampering away in front of me and climbing the trees. It always seems that he is happy to see me, and he was never wary of the nice guy that I am, sometimes even approaching me from a distance of just two or three steps away. I often imagine that his big, dark brown eyes are smiling at me.

Unfortunately, in our country, we don't have squirrels. We have an animal called a jerboa that resembles a kangaroo puppy or a mouse. You can only hunt the jerboa by pouring water into its many burrows and waiting a moment for it to escape from the man-made typhoon that has turned its hole into a watery state of emergency—for it to jump suddenly from the muddy burrow and run away. The jerboa is an intelligent rodent, but the squirrel is beautiful, kind, and happy. True, the Libyan jerboa does not care about date pits and eats other things, but, to be honest, its meat is delicious when grilled. Moreover, folk doctors and fortune tellers at the Albaladi hotel bazaar in Benghazi say that the jerboa meat is a medicine for many chronic and dangerous diseases.

Jerboas in my country have miserable luck and never enjoy any comfort. They are always being pursued by both professional and amateur hunters, among them those who desire the jerboa meat for food or medicine and others who hunt it for nothing more than enjoyment. The jerboas are always raising their tiny hands to the sky, asking for protection, but only more hunters come. Perhaps one day the jerboa will become extinct because of this unjust hunting that is also, on paper, forbidden by the forest protection apparatus. However, in reality, you only hear the shouts and exclamations of the hunters, saying to one another, "Grab the jerboa . . . It's getting away . . . It escaped from there . . . No, from there!"

The investigator said to me, "Whatever you are thinking about, son, don't worry. Your problem is very simple."

I told him, "The squirrel's eyes reminded me of an animal in our country that resembles it called the jerboa. It is an oppressed animal with bad luck because it doesn't live here, where it could scavenge for hazelnuts, almonds, and chestnuts. Anyhow, let's return to the original topic: the habit of tossing the date pits makes me happy, and I would not like to stop it. If I were to stop doing it on a daily basis, my mental health would be very damaged. Our family doctor knows that, and I have a file concerning dates in the archives of her clinic. This is the ritual that makes it possible for me to tolerate homesickness and life in exile. If you forbid me from doing this thing that I love, I will complain about you to human rights organizations, civil societies, the Green Party, the Christian Party, the Socialist Party, the Leftist Party, as well as the organization for the protection of squirrels. Moreover, I will complain to all of the churches of Germany. Really, there is nothing in this beautiful country that gives me more joy than the dates and their pits that I toss on the grass and mud. If you wish for me to stop tossing the pits, I will do so reluctantly and deal with the pain, but if some unpleasant thing were to happen, you all would bear the responsibility."

The investigator said to me, "Don't worry. Your happiness and health are important to us. I'll make a deal with you for the sake of your mental health and this habit you love so much. Providing psychological comfort for the refugee is among the priorities of our municipality, and we must vigorously support this priority. The German taxpayers would be very happy if their money went toward making someone happy who is otherwise depressed and miserable because he is far from his homeland. As long as the pits are picked up by the squirrels, and the pits are not piling up and causing any environmental pollution, we will allow you to continue tossing them. We are going to write a permit for you to toss the pits, so toss them as you please, *our dear guest*. However, if the pits begin to pile up, we will kindly forbid you to do so, and if you resist, we will use the force of the law. What do you think?"

I bumped his fist with my fist and said to him, "*Ya deen immi!* Heck yeah bro, I agree!"

After obtaining the permit, I began gleefully tossing the pits. My mouth would chew the dates, taking pleasure in the sweetness, and my hand would dispose of the pits slowly, as if sowing a seed. As for my spirits, they were intoxicated by this action to the utmost degree.

In the evenings, I sit on the balcony drinking a cup of coffee or a glass of alcohol, usually wine or Italian grappa. I imagine that the grappa is actually Benghazi grappa (double distilled), taking me back to the country and all its worries and craziness. In front of me is the horizon stretched out and ending at the snow-capped mountains, and I see the scenes of Benghazi that I love: the sea waves along the Benghazi corniche; the cathedral with its two magnificent domes like two bosoms ready to nurse the sky; the Sidi Khrebish lighthouse; the Tree Square; the Julyana summer resort; the Albaladi hotel bazaar; Bugula Street and the Jareed and Thalaam markets; July 23 Park and Gamal Abdel Nasser Street; Cafe Labda; the barber Maziq; Sports City; the Albaraka neighborhood; the Sidi Hussein neighborhood with the restaurant Hamidu Fasuliya and my many friends there, especially my friend Alhameed Qays and his father Hussein Qarquum Hayta, whose sense of humor makes me live in a state of continual laughter; and the Almuheeshi neighborhood where I lived before departing for Germany.

I drink and eat dates, calmly tossing the pits down below. On the floor below us lives a Syrian family that loves roses and is always putting red flower pots on the balcony. On the ground floor lives a Yemeni family with whom we have a good and solid relationship. They are always sending us Yemeni food, and when it is our turn, we send them Libyan food. They will send us a meal of long rice mixed with strips of potatoes and chicken drumsticks, and we will send them a meal of short rice mixed with pumpkin, zucchini, carrots, green beans, hummus, potatoes, mutton, and, of course, fried red bell peppers. As for the Syrian family, they are always sending us bak-lava, knafeh, basbousa, ma'amoul (date cookies), appetizers, and various salted, pickled vegetables. In return, we send them makroudh (cookies filled with dates and nuts), cake, algareeba (sugar cookies), sfinz (spongy fried bread), zalabiyeh (fritters), olive oil, and harissa.

The neighbors—God bless them—are good people. Even if a date pit strays from its course and heads toward the park grass, or if the wind pushes it onto the balcony of the Syrians, Yemenis, or other families, they wouldn't file a complaint against me. Instead, they would return the dear, revered pit to me on a plate or in a small cup so that I may launch it again the next time. Indeed, they understand me—may God keep them well and make them happy—and they know that tossing the pits allows me to forget my homesickness and pain. The first time that I dropped a pit onto their balcony, I apol-ogized to them, saying, "Whoever among you has not sinned may throw a date at me."

They laughed, and the head of their family said to me, "No wor-ries—if only all of the shots that hit me were dates."

Date Palms

After a while, a few date pits sprouted. Seedlings taking the shape of green legs burst forth in several locations on the ground surrounding our building. The green legs were draped with green feathers on both sides that later transformed into palm leaves. Perhaps the squirrels were on a vacation, or they migrated to another place, and so they didn't come to pick up more pits, and those pits germinated. Maybe the squirrels themselves planted the pits by burying them in the dirt for the purpose of storage, just as they do with the hazelnuts and other types of nuts. Maybe they got the pits wet with saliva, which acted as a sort of irrigation, or they urinated or defecated on the dirt where they had buried the pits, and this organic fertilizer gave the pits the strength to sprout upward toward the sun.

The days preceding the discovery of my beautiful plants were hot, to the point where we started to smell the odor of something emanating from the ground after being still and frozen during the cold. The weather of those days was similar to the climate in northern Africa, and it made all of Europe complain about a heat wave. Due to the melting snow on top of the mountains, flooding occurred, and the water level of many rivers rose and submerged buildings and houses on the riverbanks. Moreover, some deaths occurred among older people and children due to the rising temperatures, and many animals died due to an outbreak of forest fires, a result of the madness that nature metes out on our planet from time to time. In those days, some people began walking nearly naked in the streets. The ice cream shops were crowded with lickers, and the public pools were also more packed than I had ever seen them before. The ground beneath us felt a bit warm, perhaps from the central heating lines for the ground-floor apartments or from an underground spring that had been motionless but was now furiously bubbling. Honestly, I didn't care about the reason; I was just overjoyed that the pits succeeded in sprouting in a climate that was not their native weather and soil that was not their native soil. These pits were like an immigrant who strives to acclimate to an environment that is not his or her native environment, trying to blend in by learning the language and respecting the customs and laws.

Perhaps the date pits drew strength from my mouth as well, before reaching the mouth of the squirrel. The pits may have taken a little bit of my date-loving soul's yeast with them before going to sleep in the ground. There, they would be planted just as I have been planted in Germany, trying to align myself with their precise, organized manner of life. Customarily, I do not remove the pit from the date in the open air, that is, outside of my mouth. My method for eating dates is based on leisureliness: I put the date in my mouth, and inside that warm factory, the eating procedures are carried out slowly. I begin by stripping the pit of its sweet golden-brown and white clothing. Then, after making sure it has been exhausted by the caresses of my tongue, and that it has taken its share of warmth from my soul, I push it forward between my lips where my fingers gently receive it. I contemplate the pit and confirm that it is warm, alive, and full of love. Then, I send it to our Mother Earth, which will certainly not neglect it but rather provide it with means of subsistence and favorable conditions for life.

After some time, the new plants began to grow taller with confidence and enthusiasm. Their cylindrical trunks thickened from the bottom, and dense palm leaves came out from all sides. They were growing faster than German trees and plants, as if they were being nourished with a beneficial and fast-acting protein, like the ones athletes take for their bodies. Or rather, as if they were stealing the nourishment from the neighboring German trees and plants. But perhaps those trees and plants were fine with it, and they love altruism, gladly giving their nutrients to the newly arrived date palms. Maybe the generosity of plants far exceeds that of humans, or maybe there are no evil, far-right, extremist plants to obstruct the natural growth of the new plants by nipping them in the bud.

My date pits were planted in natural, favorable conditions, even better than the conditions of a greenhouse within an agricultural college. The winds from all directions supported the pits with love and warmth. Even the cold that tried to kill them was resisted; instead, the pits actually embraced it and acclimated to it. As for the autumn that strips the German trees of their leaves, it left the palm leaves as they were—tender, ripe, and green. Perhaps autumn is afraid of removing leaves from the date palm. Perhaps it won't approach palm branches to rip out their leaves for reasons of its own, and it does not desire to reveal these reasons to us. For just as winter, spring, and summer have their secrets, autumn has its own secrets as well.

My date pits were planted and became date palms. I will not search for the secret to their success in growing. They are, in the end, blessed trees, among the trees celebrated and preordained by God. Generally speaking, I don't inquire about issues related to date palms, olive trees, fig trees, or even pomegranate trees. I feel that something spiritual protects those trees from conditions of nature, human oppression, insect abuse, and diseases.

I was pleased with their actions, their willfulness, and their resilience in the face of harsh nature. Thank God, I finally had a homeland. I finally had a date palm oasis close to me, and every day I would watch the oasis palms swaying rhythmically together, they singing to me and I singing to them. However, as usual in my bewildering life, through which I have suffered, my elation didn't last for long. Soon thereafter the Ministry of Agriculture, which came by routinely to prune trees and mow the lawns of our neighborhood parks, discovered the foreign trees. The Ministry knew that I was the one who planted them, unintentionally, of course, but nevertheless in agreement with the municipality via the permit that was granted to me some time before. And so, of course, they summoned me urgently. They gave me the choice between uprooting the foreign trees that I had planted by tossing the pits or moving the trees to a nursery with other trees belonging to the agricultural college in the city. There, the date palms could join a diverse group of plants from around the world, and they would be observed by tourists and studied by students of agriculture, pharmacy, and alternative medicine, especially in matters connected to the ability of the date palms to germinate and live in a non-native environment.

The Ministry of Agriculture would pay me a reward for my effort in cultivating the date palms, but I refused. I quickly went to the municipality and filed a complaint. The real estate company supported me, saying, "As long as the Libyan tenant is linked to us by an official contract, and for years he has been regular in paying rent, heat, and maintenance fees, he has total freedom to plant any plants he desires in the yards belonging to the real estate company, with the exception of poisonous plants or drug-producing plants such as poppy seeds. Regarding the date palms, these are legal trees under no uncertain terms."

All of the neighbors were delighted that many date palms would be planted around the building in the future, and they pledged to care for my little palms, even without my requesting them to do so. The neighbors placed charming little clay circles around the palms to prevent them from getting trampled, and they did not allow children to play nearby. Even the squirrels, after returning, found that what they had buried for later use had sprung up as palm trees, and they did not harm the palm roots or leaves. Instead, they seemed cheerful, circling around the palms and trying to climb up. Of course, the squirrels continued their pastime of taking the charity that I tossed. On more than one occasion, I noticed that they would take a pit and wouldn't bury it in the dirt but rather ascend to the treetops and store it there inside of a narrow crack they had made in the bark.

The senior citizens would look out of their windows and balconies, observing the foreign trees in the park across from their nursing home. On their strolls in the afternoons, they would ask the nurses to push their wheelchairs near these trees to take a closer look. They took great delight in watching as the squirrels danced around the trees and tried to climb up, unafraid of piercing the braided outer layer of the palm tree. When the elderly people discovered that I was observing them from my balcony, they would wave hello, and I would ask my young daughter to go down right away with a plate of Libyan dates that had recently arrived from Fezzan, Jalu, or Aljala. My daughter would distribute the dates as if passing out candy. The *Deglet* date is very moist, with no need for chewing. Each elderly person would take one date. Some enjoyed sucking it down as if it were warm ice cream; some said that they first needed a doctor's permission, but they would store it in a drink or biscuit container that was with them; and others extracted the pit from the date and then placed the date in a bun or between two biscuits, eating it with afternoon tea. With each bite they would smile and look at the date palms with leaves being moved by the wind.

The date palms grew quickly. The ground became their home, and the sky welcomed their height. As for their roots, they expanded and spread out comfortably to the depths of the earth, with twisted lanes in every direction. The roots tried to fix themselves well in the soil that was previously unfamiliar to those particular roots and their genes. The roots tried to reach beneficial ground nutrients different from those that come from the rainy sky, which provides irrigation. The roots were searching for natural warmth from below, searching for a hot sun that was not deceptive like the one that rose upon them each morning but was empty of warmth, emitting cold rays of light and nothing more.

Roots

The asphalt road that ran between us, the church, and the nursing home began to crack. One wide crack looked like a trench, splintering in the middle, with other small cracks spreading out to the sides. The cracks began to fill with water, and they damaged cars, passersby, motorcycle riders, and the like. Even children on skates were hurt, with one child stumbling on the trench and bruising his knees and elbows. A nursing home team was vigilant, pushing wheelchairs gently when they approached the cracks, so that no elderly person would hurt their brittle bones. Naturally, many complaints were raised because of the cracks, especially from those driving fancy cars to drop off their kids at the international school each morning and pick them up in the afternoon.

It was on a weekend when the construction workers suddenly came in their vehicles to inspect the road. They took photographs of the road as well as a sample of the cracked asphalt. Two hours later, a company came with its equipment to repair the road, and thus began the work to treat the cracks. They had only dug about half a meter down when they came upon the roots of a date palm that had stretched out in the dirt like an interwoven chain beneath the workers. The workers began to use their tractor to carefully pull apart the roots without breaking them, altering the direction of the roots toward the vegetable garden and the mother date palm. The workers used caution in dealing with the roots, as if they were arteries carrying blood. Instructions had been given for them to be cautious while digging and to treat with kindness any plant or creature residing underground.

The company engineer who was supervising the workers began to take pictures of the roots that caused the cracks while also taking samples of the surrounding soil and the soil stuck to the roots so it could be analyzed. Then, she ordered the workers to dig to a depth of two meters in order to fix the road properly and to not allow the cracking to return, no matter how much weight was put on the asphalt and no matter how hard it rained. The workers began their digging, without causing any damage to the plants. They had made good progress, but when they wanted to execute the engineer's instructions and go deeper, the bucket of the backhoe struck the body of a metallic object, sending out a ring like that of the church bells. The workers immediately stopped digging and called the engineer, who was sipping coffee at the buffet cart next to the company equipment, and she hurried over immediately. She used a metal scraper with rough teeth like a comb to wipe the surface of the metallic object, discovering some letters on its body. She called the police, army, fire department, and hospital. The metallic object was, in fact, a huge, old bomb appearing to date back to World War II. Soon thereafter, a state of emergency was announced in the city, and the secure neighborhood was transformed into what resembled an active military barracks teeming with soldiers, weapons, and vehicles with advanced electronic equipment. Residential neighborhoods and businesses surrounding the bomb hole were evacuated, and the roads heading into the neighborhood were closed. The seniors were transported by ambulances to other centers of accommodation, and the municipality took responsibility for the building residents, opening up a number of schools for them in other neighborhoods so that they could rest until the dangerous threat to their lives was over. The nuns and clergymen from the two churches preferred to remain with the army and police to pray. As for the tall policewoman with the blonde braids, given that the incident had occurred in her neighborhood, she was standing directly at the mouth of the hole, assisting the specialists in deactivating the bomb. After two hours of exhausting, meticulous work, the deactivation of the bomb that looked like a small missile was complete. The bomb weighed more than two kantars (about two hundred pounds). Fortunately, it never exploded throughout the dozens of years it spent sleeping underground, perhaps because it fell between the two churches. Each church had nursed the congregations with the milk of peace and security, and later the nursing home was built, with those powerless seniors safeguarded by Jesus and his disciples.

The bomb was extracted by a crane belonging to the civil defense. They placed it with great care and caution on a special military truck and took it out of the area. All types of media were present, and the journalists took many photographs. Satellite TV channels conducted numerous interviews with the city mayor, the police, and leaders of the bomb squad, in addition to some members of the fire department, ambulance crews, civil defense, and the lead engineer who discovered the bomb. After that, the road workers resumed their work, residents were permitted to return to their homes, and the elderly were permitted to return to the nursing home. They were all very happy, and everyone gave thanks to the date palms. If not for the blessing of their roots, the bomb would not have been discovered. The director of the nursing home suggested that the elderly residents themselves present a valuable gift to whomever it was that planted the date palms of peace.

Contributors

Sara Abou Rashed is a Palestinian American poet and storyteller. Her works appear in *Poetry, Poetry Wales, Arab Lit Quarterly,* and the anthology *A Land with a People* and English high school curriculum from McGraw Hill. She has been nominated for a Pushcart Prize and named a Poetry Fellow at the Vermont Studio Center. Since 2018, Sara has performed her autobiographical one-woman show, *A Map of Myself: My Odyssey to America,* over 17 times across the United States. She is currently pursuing her MFA at the University of Michigan. More at www.saraabourashed.com and www.mapofmyself.com.

Nisma Alaklouk is a Brussels-based Palestinian author of plays, novels, and short stories. Her work has been published in Arabic and Dutch and translated into French and English. The story translated here, "Hiyya, Huwwa, wa-Ghazzah," originally appeared in *Hādhihi Laysat Ḥaqībah* (This is not a suitcase), a collection of stories by Arab writers living in Belgium.

Mohamad Alasfar was born in Libya in 1960 and grew up in the city of Benghazi. Before his writing career began in the late 1990s, al-Asfar spent time working as a teacher in elementary and middle schools; as a professional footballer; and as a traveling salesman, visiting many countries throughout Asia, Europe, and the Middle East. As a writer, Alasfar has been published in most Libyan publications and in literary websites, international magazines, and global newspapers, including the *New York Times*. His novels and short story collections have been published by various publishing houses in Lebanon, Syria, Libya, Tunisia, Jordan, Egypt, and the United Kingdom. His short story "The Story of a Sock" was turned into a short film and won the creativity prize at the 2013 Cairo Short Film Festival.

Marilyn Booth is Khalid bin Abdallah Al Saud Professor for the Study of the Contemporary Arab World, University of Oxford. Her recent monograph, *The Career and Communities of Zaynab Fawwaz: Feminist Thinking in* Fin-de-siècle *Egypt* (2021), is among her numerous publications on early feminism, translation, and Arabophone women's writing in Egypt and Ottoman Syria. Initiator of the Ottoman Translation Studies Group, she edited *Migrating Texts: Circulating Translations around the Ottoman Mediterranean* (2019) and is co-editing a second volume of this collective's research. She has translated 18 published works of fiction and memoir from Arabic, most recently, Hoda Barakat's *Voices of the Lost* and Hassan Daoud's *No Road to Paradise.* She was co-winner of the 2019 Man Booker International Prize for her translation of Jokha Alharthi's *Celestial Bodies.* Her translation of Alharthi's novel *Bitter Orange Tree* is coming out in May 2022. She hopes to translate Dost's *Safe Corridor* and is looking for a publisher.

Muhammad Diab is a Syrian writer.

Jan Dost, born in 1965, is a native of Kobani, in the Aleppo region of Syria. A student of natural sciences at the University of Aleppo, he embarked on a career in journalism as both reporter and editor. His novels (composed in Arabic or in Kurdish) have been translated into Spanish, Turkish, Arabic, Kurdish, Persian, and Italian. He has received numerous awards in Syria (Short Story Prize, 1992), the Kurdistan Region of Iraq (Hussein Arif Award for Creativity, 2014; Mem u Zin Literature Festival Award, 2021), Germany (Kurdish Poetry Prize, 2012), and Austria (Sharafnama Award for Kurdish Culture, 2021). He has published five novels in Kurdish and seven in Arabic, as well as four volumes of poetry; he has translated literary works from Kurdish and Persian into Arabic and from Arabic into Kurdish. He has participated in translation workshops and conferences as well as speaking at book fairs. Since 2000, he has resided in Germany and is a German citizen.

Michael Fares is a Lebanese American software engineer, musician, and former professor. He was a Professor of Arabic at University of

Houston from 2012 to 2022, prior to which he completed his MA in Arabic with a focus on foreign language pedagogy at the University of Texas at Austin. He received his BA in History from the College of William and Mary, with a minor in philosophy. He grew up in the Middle East and has spent time in several Arabic-speaking countries.

Angela Haddad is a PhD candidate in the Department of Comparative Literature at New York University. Her research focuses on the Arab diaspora and its literary production in the Mediterranean and Caribbean. After attending the University of Michigan for her BA, she earned her MA in Arab Studies from Georgetown University and is a freelance translator from Arabic into English.

Ali Harb is a Lebanese American Washington, DC–based journalist who covers Arab American communities and US foreign policy.

Haji Jabir is an award-winning Eritrean author of five novels to date. He currently lives in Doha, Qatar, where he works as a journalist for *Al Jazeera*. One of the most significant Arabic-language authors of his time, Jabir strives in his creative work to shed light on Eritrea in the past and present and to extricate his homeland and its people from their isolation on the world stage.

Ghassan Kanafani was a Palestinian fiction writer, journalist, and leftist political thinker. One of the Arab world's most prominent modern authors, he was born in 1936 and forced to flee northern Palestine during the Nakba that preceded Israel's founding. Eventually settling in Beirut, Kanafani joined the Popular Front for the Liberation of Palestine in 1965 and later founded its political magazine *Al Hadaf*. In 1972, at the age of 36, he was assassinated in a car bomb explosion orchestrated by the Israeli Mossad. Kanafani's novels—particularly *Men in the Sun* and *Returning to Haifa*—are some of the most iconic works of Palestinian literature.

Graham Liddell is a writer, translator, and PhD candidate in Comparative Literature at the University of Michigan. His dissertation, *Wayfinding, Worldmaking*, is a study of contemporary Arab and

Afghan migration narratives in both literature and the asylum process. His translations of two short stories from Emile Habiby's collection *Sextet of the Six-Day War* were published in *Banipal* in 2022. Prior to graduate school, Liddell worked in journalism, focusing on the Arab world.

Khaled Mattawa is the William Wilhartz Professor of English Language and Literature at the University of Michigan. His latest book of poems is *Fugitive Atlas* (Graywolf, 2020). A MacArthur Fellow, he is the current editor of *Michigan Quarterly Review*.

Mootacem B. Mhiri holds a PhD in Comparative Literature and is a senior lecturer in Arabic at Vassar College, New York. Mhiri teaches Arabic language and Arabic literature in translation under the auspices of the Africana Studies Program and translates literary works from Arabic to English and English to Arabic. His work has appeared in *Pensive: A Global Journal of Spirituality and the Arts* and in *Making Mirrors: Writing/Righting by Refugees* (translated by Mootacem Mhiri, edited by Becky Thompson and Jehan Bseiso).

Rachid Niny is a journalist, editor, and founding member of the daily newspaper *Al Massae* from Morocco. He is a graduate of the University of Literature and Human Sciences in Mohammedia and has collaborated with *Al Alam* and *Assabah*. In April of 2011, he was arrested for his writings and served a one-year sentence, during which he was awarded the Oxfam Novib/PEN award.

Gulala Nouri is a renowned Kurdish Iraqi poet, fiction writer, and translator. She is a recipient of HOMER—The European Medal of Poetry and Art, among other literary awards. Her 2011 translations of Vladimir Vysotsky's poetry from Russian into Kurdish and Arabic earned international acclaim. Nouri mostly writes in Arabic and has published multiple volumes of poetry and short story collections. She currently resides in Dearborn, Michigan, and has previously lived in California.

Nancy Roberts is a freelance Arabic-to-English translator and editor with experience in the areas of modern Arabic literature, politics, and education; international development; Arab women's economic and political empowerment; Islamic jurisprudence and theology; Islamist thought and movements; and interreligious dialogue. Literary translations include works by Ghada Samman, Ahlem Mosteghanemi, Naguib Mahfouz, Ibrahim Nasrallah, Ibrahim al-Koni, Salman al-Farsi, Laila Aljohani, and Haji Jabir, among others. Her translation of Ghada Samman's *Beirut '75* (University of Arkansas Press, 1995) won the 1994 Arkansas Arabic Translation Award; her rendition of Salwa Bakr's *The Man from Bashmour* (AUC Press, 2007) was awarded a commendation in the 2008 Saif Ghobash Banipal Prize for Translation, while her English translations of Ibrahim Nasrallah's *Gaza Weddings* (Hoopoe Press, 2017), *The Lanterns of the King of Galilee* (AUC Press, 2015), and *Time of White Horses* (Hoopoe Reprint, 2016) won her the 2018 Sheikh Hamad Award for Translation and International Understanding. She is based in Wheaton, Illinois.

Julia Schwartz completed her MA in Arabic for Professional Purposes at the University of Michigan in April 2022. Before starting her master's program, she taught English in Morocco for three years while studying Moroccan Darija in her free time. She is spending the 2022–2023 academic year as a CASA Fellow in Amman.

Becky Thompson is the author of *To Speak in Salt*, winner of the Ex Ophidia Poetry Book Prize. Also a scholar and activist, she has written, among other books, *Teaching with Tenderness* and *Survivors on the Yoga Mat* and has co-edited two poetry anthologies, including *Making Mirrors: Writing/Righting by and for Refugees* (with Jehan Bseiso). Her honors include the Gustavus Myers Award for Outstanding Books on Human Rights and fellowships from the Rockefeller Foundation and the National Endowment for the Humanities. She has held appointments at China Women's University, Princeton University, Duke University, the University of Colorado, and, currently, Simmons University. She greatly appreciates Mootacem Mhiri's translations of her poetry.

James Vizthum is a PhD candidate in the Department of Middle East Studies at the University of Michigan. His research in the field of Applied Arabic Linguistics focuses on the processes of written word recognition by adult learners of Arabic. He has taught Arabic courses at the University of Michigan and the Middlebury College Summer Arabic Program.

Saadi Youssef (1934–2021) is considered one of the most important contemporary poets in the Arab world. He was born near Basra, Iraq. Following his experience as a political prisoner in Iraq, he spent most of his life in exile, working as a teacher and literary journalist throughout North Africa and the Middle East. He is the author of over 40 books of poetry. Youssef also published two novels and a book of short stories and several essay collections and memoirs. He spent the last two decades of his life in London and was a leading translator to Arabic of works by Walt Whitman, Ngugi wa Thiongo, and Federico García Lorca, among many others.

Sources

Alaklouk, Nisma. "Hiyya, huwwa, wa-Ghazzah" [Her, him, and Gaza]. In *Hadhihi Laysat Ḥaqībah* [This is not a suitcase], edited by Ṭaha ʿAdnān, 131–141. Casablanca: Editions La Croisée des Chemins, 2016.

Alasfar, Mohamad. *Tamr wa-Qaʿmūl* [Dates and wild artichokes]. Amman: Dar al-Jaidah, 2019.

Diab, Muhammad. "Muktāʾib fī ʾAlmāniyā . . . Yaktashif al-ʾAlam wa-Yurāsil Gharībah fi-l-Manām" [A depressed Syrian . . . discovers pain and contacts a stranger in a dream]. *Al Modon*, July 14, 2020. https://bit.ly/3AO8KRm.

———. "Yawmiyyāt Muktaʾib Sūrī fī ʾAlmāniyā" [Diary of a depressed Syrian in Germany]. *Al Modon*, June 19, 2020. https://bit.ly/3e9egpR.

Dost, Jan. *Mimarr ʾĀmin* [Safe corridor]. Tunis: Meskiliani Publishing, 2019.

Jabir, Haji. *Marsā Fāṭimah* [Fatima's harbor]. Beirut: Al-Markaz ath-Thaqāfī al-ʿArabī, 2013.

Kanafani, Ghassan. "The Stolen Shirt." *Jadaliyya*, March 31, 2015. Translated by Michael Fares. https://www.jadaliyya.com/Details/31937.

Niny, Rachid. *Yawmiyyāt Muhājir Sirrī* [Journal of a clandestine migrant]. Rabat: Editions Okad, 2006.

Thompson, Becky. *To Speak in Salt*. Seattle: Ex Ophidia Press, 2022.

Youssef, Saadi. *Qaṣāʾid Hayrfīld at-Tall* [Poems of Harefield on the Hill]. Cologne: Manshūrāt al-Jamal, 2013.

www.ingramcontent.com/pod-product-compliance
Lightning Source LLC
Chambersburg PA
CBHW060328260626
47160CB00007B/2723